937
MAT

DATE DUE

FEB 0 1 2004	
DEC 26 2006	
FEB 03 2007	
APR 02 2007	

DEMCO INC 38-2971

DAILY LIFE OF

THE ANCIENT ROMANS

The Greenwood Press "Daily Life Through History" Series

The Ancient Egyptians
Bob Brier and Hoyt Hobbs

The Ancient Greeks
Robert Garland

Ancient Mesopotamia
Karen Rhea Nemet-Nejat

The Aztecs: People of the Sun and Earth
David Carrasco with Scott Sessions

Chaucer's England
Jeffrey L. Singman and Will McLean

Civil War America
Dorothy Denneen Volo and James M. Volo

Colonial New England
Claudia Durst Johnson

18th-Century England
Kirstin Olsen

Elizabethan England
Jeffrey L. Singman

The Holocaust
Eve Nussbaum Soumerai and Carol D. Schulz

The Inca Empire
Michael A. Malpass

The Italian Renaissance
Elizabeth S. Cohen and Thomas V. Cohen

Maya Civilization
Robert J. Sharer

Medieval Europe
Jeffrey L. Singman

The Nineteenth Century American Frontier
Mary Ellen Jones

The United States, 1940–1959: Shifting Worlds
Eugenia Kaledin

The United States, 1960–1990: Decades of Discord
Myron A. Marty

Victorian England
Sally Mitchell

DAILY LIFE OF
THE ANCIENT ROMANS

DAVID MATZ

The Greenwood Press "Daily Life Through History" Series

GREENWOOD PRESS
Westport, Connecticut • London

Library of Congress Cataloging-in-Publication Data

Matz, David.
  Daily life of the ancient Romans / David Matz.
      p. cm.—(The Greenwood Press "Daily life through history" series,
  ISSN 1080–4749)
  Includes bibliographical references and index.
  ISBN 0–313–30326–6 (alk. paper)
  1. Rome—Social life and customs. 2. Rome—Civilization. I. Title. II. Series.
DG78.M385 2002
937—dc21   2001018220

British Library Cataloguing in Publication Data is available.

Library of Congress Catalog Card Number: 2001018220
ISBN: 0–313–30326–6
ISSN: 1080–4749

First published in 2002

Greenwood Press, 88 Post Road West, Westport, CT 06881
An imprint of Greenwood Publishing Group, Inc.
www.greenwood.com

Printed in the United States of America

The paper used in this book complies with the
Permanent Paper Standard issued by the National
Information Standards Organization (Z39.48–1984).

10 9 8 7 6 5 4 3 2

Copyright Acknowledgment

The author and publisher gratefully acknowledge permission for use of the following
material:

Excerpts from Loeb Classical Library editions are reprinted by permission of the publishers
and the Trustees of the Loeb Classical Library, Cambridge, Mass.: Harvard University
Press. The Loeb Classical Library® is a registered trademark of the President and Fellows
of Harvard College.

Contents

A photo essay follows Chapter 6.

Chronology

ca. 1200 B.C.	Aeneas flees the burning walls of Troy and begins his long sea journey culminating in Italy, where he founds a new race, the Roman people
ca. 753	Traditional founding of the city by Romulus
753–509	Seven legendary kings rule Rome, beginning with Romulus and ending with Tarquinius Superbus
509	Superbus is expelled, along with the monarchy; founding of the Roman Republic
ca. 450	Publication of the Twelve Tables, the first codification of Roman law
387	Gallic invasion of Rome
367	Lex Licinia is enacted, which opens to plebeians the office of consul (the chief governmental office of the Republic, formerly held exclusively by patricians)
late 4th century	Samnite wars
ca. 312	Construction begins on the most famous Roman road, the Via Appia, or Appian Way
279	Battle of Asculum against King Pyrrhus, who, although victorious, lost so many soldiers that he supposedly remarked that another such triumph would be his undoing; hence, the first "Pyrrhic victory"

264–241	First Punic War
218–201	Second Punic War
218	In one of the most amazing feats in ancient history, the Carthaginian general Hannibal crosses the trackless, snow-swept Alps Mountains along with his army and their pack animals, including several dozen elephants
ca. 204	The production of one of Plautus's best known comedies, *Miles Gloriosus* (The Bragging Soldier), which was the basis for the modern stage play and film *A Funny Thing Happened on the Way to the Forum*
184	Cato the Elder, one of Rome's most famous statesmen/politicians, holds the office of censor
149–146	Third Punic War; destruction of Carthage
144	Construction begins on Rome's first high-level aqueduct, the Aqua Marcia (Marcian Aqueduct)
133	Tiberius Sempronius Gracchus holds the office of tribune; his sponsorship of a controversial land redistribution plan ultimately leads to his violent death in a riot, the first time that Roman blood is shed in a civil disturbance
104–100	Gaius Marius holds an unprecedented five consecutive consulships (he also served as consul in 107 and 86)
100	Birth of Gaius Julius Caesar
70	Birth of Publius Vergilius Maro (Vergil), author of the *Aeneid*
63	Cicero's consulship; his denunciation of Catiline and the Catilinarian conspiracy
63	Birth of the future emperor Augustus
59	Julius Caesar's consulship
58–50	Julius Caesar's Gallic governorship; his memoirs, *The War in Gaul*, achieved lasting fame as a reading staple for second-year Latin classes
49–45	Civil war
44	March 15, Caesar's assassination
44–31	Civil war
31	Battle of Actium: defeat of the naval forces of Cleopatra and Mark Antony by Augustus
27	Augustus finishes consolidating his power; transition from Republic to Empire

27–A.D. 14	Augustus rules Rome as its first emperor
A.D. 54–68	Reign of emperor Nero, who supposedly "fiddled while Rome burned" in the devastating conflagration of 64
69	Four different men (Galba, Otho, Vitellius, Vespasian) rule Rome; hence, A.D. 69 is commonly known as the Year of the Four Emperors
79	Eruption of Mount Vesuvius, which buries the cities of Pompeii and Herculaneum; the youthful Pliny the Younger saw it happen and later wrote two descriptive letters about the event to the historian Tacitus
80	Completion of the Flavian Amphitheater (Coliseum) in Rome
96–180	The reigns of the five so-called Good Emperors: Nerva, Trajan, Hadrian, Antoninus Pius, and Marcus Aurelius
180–285	Chaotic times, with a succession of little-known or not-long-remembered emperors—with one or two exceptions, such as Caracalla (reigned 211–217), famous in part for the elaborate public bathing establishment that bears his name
285	The reign of emperor Diocletian begins, and with it, the Late Roman Empire
301	The promulgation of the Edict of Diocletian, a wage-price freeze
324–337	Constantine the Great rules as Rome's first Christian emperor
354	Birth of St. Augustine, perhaps the most influential Christian writer and theologian of any age
395	Christianity is now established as the state religion
410	Sack of Rome by Alaric and the Visigoths
476	Rome's last emperor—the ironically named Romulus Augustulus—is deposed by the Germanic general Odoacer; end of the western Roman Empire

Introduction

I originally intended to write a book whose focus would be primarily (if not exclusively) on the common people of ancient Rome. Little or no attention would be devoted to people like Caesar or Antony, Vergil or Cicero—figures whose curricula vitae are overly familiar to legions of students of life in the ancient Roman world. A book about the Roman common people would distinguish itself by occupying a unique niche in the "daily life" pantheon. Unfortunately, that book has yet to be written.

Try as one might, it is virtually impossible to compose any kind of book-length study of any aspect of Roman civilization without sooner or later encountering—and ultimately incorporating—the writings of ancient Rome's well-known authors, playwrights, and poets. They have a knack for charging over even the sturdiest of "Famous Romans: Keep Out" signs that an author might want to figuratively post on an emerging manuscript.

So the finished product has evolved as something of a compromise. True, noted names and famous families have found their way into these pages, but I hope that many Romans heretofore cloaked in anonymity have been able to shed that confining apparel and attain their own brief moment of fame within this book.

PLAN, NATURE, AND SCOPE OF THE WORK

The book is divided into eleven chapters. The emphases of the chapters (education; slavery; food and dining; housing; travel; politics; family life;

holidays and leisure activities; sports and amusements; religion; and retirement) cumulatively paint a reasonably accurate portrait of what it
meant to be a typical ancient Roman.

Each chapter begins with a brief introduction to the topic under consideration. These introductions are brief by design; it is hoped that the
reader will learn about the chapter topics not through my contemporary
prose but through the writings and actions of the ancient Romans themselves. These writings and actions are presented in the form of individual
entries, most of which are headed by titles. The content of each entry
has been derived from an ancient source or sources, which are identified
within the text. No attempt has been made to prejudice the reader by
offering value judgments on the validity or credibility of the entries or
their sources. Although certain ancient authors do enjoy a more favorable reputation among modern critics than others, the contention here is
that all have something to contribute to our overall knowledge of life in
ancient Rome. To that extent, at least, their work is worthy of inclusion
in an effort such as this one.

**Sources and
Abbreviations**
The works of ancient authors have been the major
sources of information for this book. For a further look
at the ancient authors, the reader should look to the ap-
pendix at the back of the book; it includes brief biographies along with a listing of the author's major works. A reference list
is provided at the end of each chapter. A bibliographic essay is included
at the end of the book to provide the reader with a list of modern authors.

Other sources that were used in the preparation of this book are ab-
breviated as follows:

CIL: *Corpus Inscriptionum Latinarum,* the massive collection of Latin inscriptions.

LCL: *Loeb Classical Library,* a collection of translated works of most of the major
   Greek and Roman authors, with the English translation appearing on odd-
   numbered pages, facing the text in the original language on the even-
   numbered pages.

OCD: *Oxford Classical Dictionary,* a reference work on classical antiquities.

OLD: *Oxford Latin Dictionary.*

**Matters
Chronological**
Was life in ancient Rome in 450 B.C. any different from
life in 264 B.C.? Or 133 B.C.? Or 49 B.C.? Or A.D. 98? Of
course it was. However, a book in the "daily life" genre
must consider the "big picture"—or at least a bigger picture than simply one year or one generation. Whenever possible, individual entries are dated so that the reader has a chronological context in

which to place each entry. Most of the entries fall within the period 500 B.C. to A.D. 100; a very few stray beyond those boundaries.

Whenever an author employs the topical organiza-
tion of material, difficult editorial decisions occasion-   **Matters Topical**
ally must be made about the appropriate placement of
some entries. Attentive readers will no doubt observe instances of entries
that may seem more suited to chapters other than the ones in which they
currently appear. It is my hope instances occur infrequently.

The modern reader may not be familiar with words
like *sestertium, praenomen,* or *censor*. Rather than defin-   **Unusual Words**
ing these and similar words in the text each time they
appear—which would be a well-intentioned effort but one that would
create unnecessarily dysphonic sentences—most of these words are defined here in the Introduction.

Some Roman names have variant forms or spell-
ings. Notable examples are mentioned here.   **Variant Forms of**
                                                             Certain Names
The name of the author of the *Aeneid* is sometimes
spelled Virgil, sometimes Vergil. The latter spelling
appears in this book. Similarly, Heracles and Hercules. Again, the latter
has been used.

The correct Roman form of the name of Cleopatra's most famous par-
amour is Marcus Antonius. Thanks to Shakespeare and Hollywood,
however, he is much better known today as Mark Antony, so it is by
that name that he is referred to in this book. Other members of the Antonius family who find their way into these pages bear the Roman form
of the name: Antonius.

The Roman emperor Augustus did not actually receive that title until
27 B.C. References to Augustus prior to that time would more accurately
appear as Octavianus. (If an author really wants to be historically accurate, he or she would have to call him Octavius prior to 44 B.C., Octavianus or Octavian from 44 to 27, and Augustus thereafter. The man
did undergo several name changes.) The present volume sacrifices precision on the altar of clarity in the matter of Augustan nomenclature; he
is called Augustus throughout.

BASIC FACTS ABOUT ANCIENT ROME

In Rome's earliest days, two broad categories of
citizens were identified: patricians and plebeians. *Pa-*   **Class Distinctions**
tricians might be described as the "haves" of Roman
society, for they were generally the people who had money, property,
power, and perhaps most important, the right family connections. *Plebeians*, on the other hand, were for the most part the antitheses of patri-

cians: not as much money, property, or power, and weaker family influence. Over time, some plebeians and plebeian families climbed the socioeconomic ladder, but the ascent was usually a difficult one.

In the third and second centuries B.C., a prosperous "middle class," the *equestrian*, began to emerge. Eventually many equestrians became persons of influence in Roman society, primarily because of their wealth and commercial interests.

These class distinctions were keenly felt throughout Roman history. In politics, for example, it was extremely difficult for a *novus homo*, "new man"—one from a family that had never produced important elected officials—to strive successfully for high office. Two of the most prominent "new men" to make it all the way to the consulship were Cato the Elder, in 195 B.C., and Cicero, in 63 B.C. (An instructive contrast: new men were perceived as the opposites of *nobiles*, "known men"; hence the English words *noble* and *nobles*, which connote much the same for us today as did the word *nobiles* for the ancient Romans.)

Hail, Caesar! Roman history can be broadly divided into three periods: the *monarchy* (753–509 B.C.), the *Republic* (509–27 B.C.), and the *Empire* (27 B.C.–A.D. 476). Some disagreement exists among historians over the exact date of the fall of the Republic. The date 27 B.C. is chosen here because in that year the transition between Republic and Empire was formally recognized by the Roman political establishment, with the conferral upon Augustus of certain authoritarian powers.

During the monarchy the city was ruled by the following seven kings; dates of their reigns are close approximations:

Romulus, 753–714 B.C.

Numa Pompilius, 714–671

Tullus Hostilius, 671–642

Ancus Martius, 642–617

Tarquinius Priscus, 617–579

Servius Tullius, 579–535

Tarquinius Superbus, 535–509

After expulsion of the last king the Roman Republic was instituted, whereby the government was run by elected officials (see below, "Political Offices"). At the head were the two annually elected consuls; neither space nor scope permits a complete listing here of all the consuls, but such a list may be found in Matz's *An Ancient Rome Chronology, 264–27 B.C.* T.R.S. Broughton's *The Magistrates of the Roman Republic* offers detailed source information about individual consuls.

When the Republic fell, a one-man rule was established; even though the offices of the Republic were retained, it soon became common knowledge that the emperor controlled the government. The first nineteen (of seventy-nine total) Roman emperors were as follows:

Augustus, reigned 27 B.C.–A.D. 14	Domitian, 81–96
Tiberius, 14–37	Nerva, 96–98
Caligula, 37–41	Trajan, 98–117
Claudius, 41–54	Hadrian, 117–138
Nero, 54–68	Atoninus Pius, 138–161
Galba, 68–69	Marcus Aurelius, 161–180
Otho, 69	Lucius Verus, 161–169 (ruled with
Vitellius, 69	Marcus Aurelius)
Vespasian, 69–79	Commodus, 180–192
Titus, 79–81	Pertinax, 193

In counting years, two methods were used: the consular year, and the year from the founding of the city. Because the consulship was an annual magistracy, and because two new consuls generally assumed the office each year, these **The Roman Calendar** consular changeovers could be used as reference points for referring to a specific year. For example, in 59 B.C. the two consuls were Gaius Julius Caesar and Marcus Calpurnius Bibulus. The Romans referred to the events of that year as happening "in the consulship of Bibulus and Caesar." (The biographer Suetonius informs us that because Caesar so thoroughly overshadowed his colleague, the witty commentators of the day substituted the phrase "the consulship of Julius and Caesar.")

Rome's traditional founding date, 753 B.C., could also be used as a reference point, generally accompanied by the abbreviation A.U.C., *ab urbe condita* ("from the city's founding").

One of the reforms that Julius Caesar implemented was to base the Roman calendar on the solar year, with twelve months, 365 days, and a leap year every fourth year. This so-called Julian calendar is still the one we use today, along with a few modifications made by Pope Gregory XIII in the sixteenth century.

The twelve months of the Roman year were actually expressed adjectivally, with the name of the month used as a modifier for the noun *mensis* ("month"), thus:

mensis Januarius (January)	*mensis Julius* (July)
mensis Februarius (February)	*mensis Augustus* (August)
mensis Martius (March)	*mensis September* (September)
mensis Aprilis (April)	*mensis October* (October)

mensis Maius (May)	*mensis November* (November)
mensis Junius (June)	*mensis December* (December)

The months of July and August were originally called *mensis Quintilis* and *mensis Sextilis*, respectively, until they were renamed for Julius Caesar and Augustus. Also, the adjectives *quintilis, sextilis, september, october, november,* and *december* actually mean "fifth, sixth, seventh, eighth, ninth, and tenth [months]," a reflection of the fact that the Roman year originally began not on January 1 but on March 1.

The most unique aspect of the Roman calendar—as anyone who remembers Shakespeare, Caesar, and the Ides of March already knows—was the method used for identifying and counting the days of the month. Each month contained three reference points: the Kalends (whence our word *calendar*), the Nones, and the Ides. The Kalends was always the first day of the month, whereas the Nones might be the fifth or seventh, and the Ides the thirteenth or fifteenth, depending on the month. (In March, May, July, and October, the Nones fell on the seventh and the Ides on the fifteenth; in all other months, the Nones fell on the fifth and the Ides on the thirteenth.)

Days were identified by counting inclusively backward from the next reference point. For example, January 23 was referred to as "ten days (or the tenth day) before the Kalends of February." The entire phrase could be expressed thus: *die decimo ante Kalendas Februarias.* In practice, however, no Roman would write out such a lengthy conglomeration of words when a simple abbreviation would do just as well: *X Kal. Feb.* (Likewise, we would probably not write "January twenty-third" but rather "Jan. 23" or "1/23".)

The often-superstitious Romans viewed some days as inherently unlucky or inauspicious, as *dies nefasti*; one might equate them to contemporary uneasiness over the occasional Friday the Thirteenth. And Suetonius tells us that the emperor Augustus was leery about traveling or conducting business on the Nones of any month. Why? Because the sound of the word *Nones* bore an uncomfortably close resemblance to the Latin phrase *non is*, which means "you do not go."

Roman Currency For most of their history, the Romans used the following units of currency:

1. the *as* (pl. *asses*), a copper coin
2. the *sestertium* (pl. *sestertii*; English sesterce, sesterces), a bronze coin worth 4 *asses*
3. the *denarius* (pl. *denarii*), a silver coin worth 4 *sestertii* or 16 *asses*
4. the *aureus* (pl. *aureii*), a gold coin worth 25 *denarii*

What is this worth in American money? Given that some 2,000 years of economic, social, and political vagaries separate the modern United States from the glory of days of ancient Rome, it is impossible to provide accurate equivalencies. However, we do have some information about the buying power of these Roman coins. For example, the Edict of Diocletian, an early fourth century A.D. wage-price freeze, offers a listing of the upper wage limits for a wide variety of workers, including carpenters, wagon makers, masons, teachers, artists, camel drivers, sewer cleaners, and even shepherds; the 200 to 400 sesterce (per day) range was commonly the limit for these and similar occupations.

Would-be Roman politicians could run for a variety of offices; quaestor, aedile (but see the following para- **Political Offices** graph), praetor, consul. A politician was supposed to work his way up this ladder of offices—called the *cursus honorum*—although some skipped one or more of the rungs on the ladder. The Romans observed severe term limits: each of the four offices was to be held for one year only; re-election to the same office for a second, one-year term was rare.

The aedileship was not explicitly listed in the *cursus*, but many up-and-coming politicians ran for the office anyhow. Perhaps the best example of a traditional, "*cursus*-sensitive" career would be Cicero's: quaestor in 75 B.C., aedile in 69, praetor in 66, consul in 63. Even Julius Caesar, in many ways a revolutionary innovator, held the offices in the traditional order: quaestor in 67, aedile in 65, praetor in 62, consul in 59.

Quaestor. Quaestors were financial officials who supervised the collection of taxes and other revenues and kept track of government expenditures. Quaestors were often assigned to provinces or to the army, to oversee budgeting and payroll, and to prepare financial reports.

The number of quaestors varied dramatically. In Rome's earliest days there were only two. Their numbers gradually increased; by the time of the dictator Sulla (early first century B.C.) no fewer than twenty held office each year.

Aedile. Four aediles were chosen each year: two curule aediles, and two plebeian aediles. Although the curule aedileship apparently carried higher prestige, all four aediles had similar responsibilities: to supervise the public markets, and in particular to ensure that standard (and honest) weights and measures were used; to oversee the maintenance and cleaning of public streets as well as the maintenance and repair of temples, sewers, aqueducts, and bridges; and to inspect public baths and taverns.

Praetor. Originally there was only one praetor. But as the government bureaucracy expanded, so did the need for additional praetors. By 242 B.C. two praetors were elected annually: the *praetor urbanus*, "city praetor," and the *praetor peregrinus*, "external affairs praetor." The city praetor's primary duty was to preside over court cases involving Roman citizens, whereas the external affairs praetor handled cases between citizens and foreigners.

Around 227 the number of praetors was increased to four, and later, in 197, to six. The additional praetors were required to assist in the court and legal system and also to serve as provincial governors after their terms of office had expired.

Consul. The top spot in government—at least in the pre-imperial days—was held at one time or another by some of ancient Rome's most famous politicians, including Cato the Elder, Cicero, Pompey, Mark Antony, and Julius Caesar. Gaius Marius smashed precedent and tradition by getting himself elected consul for five consecutive terms: 104, 103, 102, 101, and 100 B.C.

Two consuls were selected annually. The consuls administered the civil government within the city, but their more important powers were military: when Rome was at war, they were the commanders-in-chief of the army.

If a consul died while in office, he was replaced in a special election by a *consul suffectus*, who would serve the remainder of the term.

Other Important Offices

Dictator. A dictator was appointed in times of national emergency, usually a military crisis; he assumed all consular powers. He was to hold office until the problem was resolved or until six months had elapsed, whichever came first. He was assisted in the fulfillment of his duties by the *magister equitum*, "master of the horse."

Tribune. The plebeians' best friends, tribunes were elected to represent and protect plebeian interests. Tribunes enjoyed several legally conferred perquisites, including *sacrosanctitas*, or personal inviolability, which theoretically granted them immunity from physical threats or harassment. They had the power to propose legislation. But their most unusual prerogative was the right of *intercessio*, or veto power, which they could exercise to nullify the proposals and enactments of other government officials, including consuls; they could also void the actions of legislative bodies. A tribune could even veto the proposals or legislative agenda of a fellow tribune. No consensus among tribunes was required; if even one, of the ten elected annually, interposed a veto, it carried full legal force.

Note: The tribunes, or more specifically "tribunes of the people," should not be confused with military tribunes, who were army officers.

Pontifex Maximus. The *pontifex maximus*, "chief priest," was the leader of the Roman religious establishment. Around the mid third century B.C. the office became an elective one, and hence politics more often than not mixed with religion in elections for this office.

Censor. The censorship was a unique office. Censors, unlike most other magistrates, were chosen only every five years; two were elected, and they served for eighteen months. Their duties were many and wide ranging: they had a general authority to examine and regulate social behavior; they could expel members of the Roman senate whose comportment or activities they deemed unworthy of a senator; they could issue nonbinding yet highly respected edicts concerning social norms; and they had the power to put up for bid contracts for the construction or repair of public works such as bridges, sewers, aqueducts, temples, and roads.

The crowning act of a censorial term of office was the preparation of a list of all Roman citizens, the *census* (hence the English word). The census, and the censors' terms, were closed by a great religious ceremony called the *lustrum*.

The Roman senate, composed roughly of 300 members, was not an elected body, and it possessed no legislative powers; rather, its function was advisory. However, because it consisted of Rome's political and financial elite, its advice on matters both domestic and foreign was usually taken seriously.

Over the course of their thousand-plus year history, the ancient Romans contended with many peoples and nations **Rome's** throughout the Mediterranean world. If the Romans could **Arch-Rival** have been polled and asked to choose the biggest rival they faced in all those years, the north African city-state of *Carthage* would almost certainly be named the most often.

Bad blood existed between the two powers since their very earliest days, when the legendary Roman hero Aeneas jilted the Carthaginian queen Dido, probably in the twelfth century B.C. Eventually the mutual animosity exploded in three hard and bitter wars, all won by the Romans:

The First Punic War, 264–241 B.C.

The Second Punic War, 218–201 B.C.

The Third Punic War, 149–146 B.C.

The second war was probably the most notable, because it featured two of the most celebrated commanders in the history of the combatants: Hannibal of Carthage, and Scipio Africanus of Rome. And many Romans would have considered the Battle of Cannae (216 B.C.) their worst-ever military defeat. On a hot August day in that year, Hannibal and the Carthaginians virtually annihilated a 60,000-man Roman force that had been sent against them.

Among the important geographical/topographical features of ancient Rome were the famed Seven Hills: (1) Pal- **Geography** atine Hill, (2) Capitoline Hill, (3) Aventine Hill, (4) Esquiline

Hill, (5) Quirinal Hill, (6) Viminal Hill, and (7) Caelian Hill. An eighth hill, the Janiculum, was located just outside the city limits.

The priciest residential sections were on the Palatine and Esquiline Hills. The Capitoline was the locale of many of the city's important temples and government buildings. The Aventine was home to many of the plebeians; it was a "middle-class" residential area.

Rome's "red-light" district, located in the central part of the city, was the *Subura*, a place where no self-respecting Roman citizen would wish to be seen, especially at night. It was frequented by muggers, thieves, murderers, and prostitutes—the dregs of Roman society—although some legitimate businesses also operated there. Its most famous resident was Julius Caesar, who lived there for a time when he first moved to Rome.

The Tiber River snakes its way through Rome, although most of the city was developed on the eastern side of the river. Rome itself was located about 15 miles from the Italian coast; its port city was Ostia, built on the mouth of the Tiber.

Rome's downtown area, the site of many a business deal, political rally, parade, or riot, was called the *forum Romanum*, or forum of Rome. Somewhere in the central city, perhaps overhanging the forum, was the gruesome cliff known as the Tarpeian Rock, a place of execution where condemned criminals were pushed over the side of the precipice.

The Roman World View The Roman's world view could probably be summarized in two words: *mare nostrum*, "our sea," which was their definition of the Mediterranean—and by extension, all the lands that bordered it. By the time the Roman Empire reached its greatest extent in the first centuries B.C. and A.D., nearly the entire Mediterranean world (and beyond) had felt the influence of Rome to some degree.

This wide sweep of Romanitas can be illustrated in many ways; perhaps one of the best would be to consider the dissemination of Roman monuments, such as amphitheaters. Some 186 amphitheaters still survive today; the most famous is the Coliseum in Rome. But these structures, or traces of them, have also been found in England, France, Germany, North Africa, Spain, Turkey, and the former Yugoslavia, not to mention in numerous locales in Italy and Sicily. Roman temples, roads, bridges, baths, and aqueducts were likewise scattered across the Mediterranean world. *Mare nostrum* was hardly an empty boast.

Today we often refer to "Roman authors," forgetting that few, if any, of them were actually born in Rome. The epigrammatist (writer of short, witty poems) Martial, for example, hailed from Spain, as did the philosopher Seneca. The comic playwright Terence was African. The poet Catullus and the historian Livy both came from northern Italy. Vergil, Ovid, Horace, and Cicero were all born in small Italian towns, out "in the middle of nowhere," as we might say today. Even St. Paul claimed Roman citizenship, and by virtue of that fact he could plausibly be called a Roman author. The city was a magnet for all manner of dramatists, historians, poets, biographers, and philosophers. In short, the word *Roman* embraced far more of the world and its people than simply those who were born within the city limits of Rome itself.

Additionally, the Romans viewed their city as a monument to perpetuity. The notion of the *urbs aeterna*, "eternal city," was well founded; after all, Rome endured and prospered for over 1,000 years. It was absolutely unthinkable that anything could ever happen to change that. So when Alaric and his Visigothic hordes invaded from the north and sacked the city in A.D. 410, it was such a shocking event that no less a figure than St. Augustine felt the need to articulate an explanation for it, and in nothing less than a book-length study (*City of God*).

This was the Roman world view—eternal city, master of the Mediterranean, home to poet and artist, orator and statesman. It is a legacy that continues to this day.

1

Education

THE ANCIENT ROMANS IN SCHOOL

In its earliest days Roman education was a family affair, with the parents of the household taking charge of their children's education. However, as Roman contacts with other parts of the Mediterranean world increased—especially, Roman shoulder-rubbing with the Greeks—a shift occurred: Roman families, at least the wealthier ones, began hiring educated Greek tutors for their children. This form of home schooling continued for centuries.

It is thought that the first elementary schools were founded in the third century B.C. These were operated on a fee-paying basis and hence were not public schools in the modern sense of the term. The teacher, or *litterator*, offered a basic curriculum of "reading and writing and arithmetic" to his young students, who typically began their studies around the age of 7.

Students who wished to advance to the next level could study literature and language under the tutelage of a *grammaticus*. These literary teachers might be independent entrepreneurs with their own schools, or they might be hired by individual families as tutors. A *grammaticus* generally worked with students no younger than the age of 12.

Additional education, in rhetoric and oratory, was available to more advanced students. For this training, however, they had to either (1) depend upon itinerant Greek teachers who visited Italy, or (2) travel to

Athens or other Greek cities where such instruction was offered. No formal rhetoric schools were opened in Italy until the third century A.D.

Schools run by *litteratores* and *grammatici* started the instructional day early—very early, sometimes before sunrise, if observers like Martial are to be believed. School "buildings" were unknown; classes met in the teacher's home, in public porticoes, or even in the streets. The students— mostly boys, although the system accepted girls also—usually brought or used wax-covered tablets, on which letters and words could be cut by using the *stilus*, a metal or wooden tool resembling a dental curette. The *stilus* featured a sharpened point at one end for "writing" and a flattened, tapered point at the other for smoothing out the wax, or "erasing." Papyrus paper, along with pen and ink, was used when available and affordable.

Much of our information about Roman education comes courtesy of the erudite and scholarly Marcus Fabius Quintilianus (better known as Quintilian, A.D. 35–100). An equally valuable source is the historian Tacitus (ca. A.D. 55–ca. 120), who eloquently describes the lessons that ought to be taught to a young child by his or her mother:

In the good old days, every man's son, born in wedlock, was brought up not in the chamber of some hireling nurse, but in his mother's lap, and at her knee. And that mother could have no higher praise than that she managed the house and gave herself to her children. Again, some elderly relative would be selected in order that to her, as a person who had been tried and never found wanting, might be entrusted the care of all the youthful scions of the same house; in the presence of such a one no base word could be uttered without grave offense, and no wrong deed done. Religiously and with the utmost delicacy she regulated not only the serious tasks of her youthful charges, but their recreations also and their games. It was in this spirit, we are told, that Cornelia, the mother of the Gracchi, directed their upbringing, Aurelia that of Caesar, Atia of Augustus: thus it was that these mothers trained their princely children. The object of this rigorous system was that the natural disposition of every child, while still sound at the core and untainted, not warped as yet by any vicious tendencies, might at once lay hold with heart and soul on virtuous accomplishments.

Tacitus goes on to compare the "good old days" with his perspective on contemporary (late first century A.D.) methods of upbringing and education:

Nowadays . . . our children are handed over at their birth to some silly little Greek serving maid, with a male slave, who may be anyone, to help her. . . . It is from the foolish tittle-tattle of such persons that the children receive their earliest impressions, while their minds are still pliant and unformed. . . . And the parents themselves make no effort to train their little ones in goodness and self- control; they grow up in an atmosphere of laxity and pertness, in which they come gradually to lose all sense of shame, and respect both for themselves and for other people. Again, there are the peculiar and characteristic vices of this metropolis of ours . . . —the passion for play actors, and the mania for gladiatorial shows and horse racing; and when the mind is engrossed in such occupations, what room is left over for higher pursuits? How few are to be found whose home-talk runs to any other subjects than these? What else do we overhear our younger men talking about whenever we enter their lecture halls? And the teachers are just as bad. With them, too, such topics supply material for gossip with their classes more frequently than any others. (Tacitus *A Dialogue on Oratory* 28; tr. Sir William Peterson LCL)

Quintilian believes it of utmost importance that a love of learning be instilled in young children in their earliest lessons, so that they will not later come to view their studies as a disagreeable chore. A teacher ought **Teaching Young Children** to be unstinting in showering young students with positive reinforcement. Stubborn or hostile students can sometimes be made less resistant if the teacher devises for his class games or competitions based on the material he wants to teach. Above all, children should be constantly encouraged, even when they falter in their studies or do not quite meet the teacher's expectations (Quintilian *Institutes of Oratory* 1.1).

Teaching a Child to Read. Quintilian admits that certain Greek authorities, such as Hesiod and Eratosthenes, suggest that children should not begin to learn to read until the age of 7; to try to instruct them in reading earlier would be futile because they would not be able to grasp the basics or "endure the strain of learning." However, Quintilian also cites the view of Chrysippus, who believed that children were capable of learning at a very young age—perhaps as early as age 3—and that "a child's mind should not be allowed to lie fallow for a moment."

Quintilian concurs. Although he also agrees that children younger than age 7 may not be efficient learners, they will still be able to absorb *something*, no matter how limited, and surely that would be preferable to *nothing*. Toddlers, like any other human beings, are mentally active during their waking hours, so why not channel at least some of that energy into learning letters? "Let us therefore not waste the earliest years. . . . The elements of literary training are solely a question of memory, which not only exists even in small children, but is specially retentive at that age" (Quintilian *Institutes of Oratory* 1.1; tr. H. E. Butler LCL).

Teaching a Child to Write. A young child could be taught to form and write letters in the following way: obtain a board and carve the letters of the alphabet into it. Then ask the child to trace the outlines of the letters with a pen or a *stilus*; it will be impossible for the young student to make mistakes, because the writing instrument will not be able to deviate from the pre-cut grooves in the board. Constant practice will enable the child to trace the letters with increasing speed and proficiency. This is desirable because "a sluggish pen delays our thoughts, while an unformed and illiterate hand cannot be deciphered" (Quintilian *Institutes of Oratory* 1.1; tr. H. E. Butler LCL).

Student Essay Contests. A teacher by the name of Marcus Verrius Flaccus (fl. first century A.D.) became famous for a method of teaching writing that he devised. He would match up students of equal ability in writing contests, having first assigned them a suitable topic. The prize offered to the winner was a rare or well-bound book. Flaccus eventually caught the eye of Augustus, who hired him as the tutor for his grandsons; in fact, Augustus invited Flaccus to move his entire school into Augustus's own expansive home, on the one condition that no more students be admitted to the school. The emperor paid Flaccus relatively well—100,000 sesterces per year—and after the teacher's death a statue of him was erected at the nearby town of Praeneste (Suetonius *On Grammarians* 17).

The Education of Cato's Son. As soon as Cato the Elder's (234–149 B.C.) son was old enough to receive instruction. Cato himself became his teacher, even though this responsibility was often assigned to educated slaves. In fact, Cato did own just such a slave, a man named Chilo, who was an experienced teacher. However, Cato did not think it appropriate for his son to be taught—or worse, corrected—by a common slave, so for that reason the young Cato did not fall under Chilo's tutelage.

First, Cato taught his son to read and to be conversant in the basic tenets of Roman law. Cato stressed physical fitness by teaching him how to throw a javelin, how to fight from horseback, how to box, and also how to survive extremes of heat and cold. Swimming formed an important part of the Catonian curriculum, and the young boy learned how to swim in the swiftly flowing Tiber River.

Cato wrote a history of Rome and used outsized letters, primarily for his son's benefit, so that the boy could become familiar with Roman history and tradition. By example he taught his son to avoid obscene language, especially in the company of women.

Cato's system must have worked, for his son grew up to be a model citizen and eventually married a lady named Tertia, a sister of Publius Cornelius Scipio Aemilianus (the Conqueror of Carthage in 146 B.C.) and a member of one of Rome's noblest families (Plutarch *Life of Cato the Elder* 20).

A Plea for Summer Vacation. Martial complains about the schoolmaster who keeps his crowd of young students busy with their studies throughout the heat of midsummer. Give them the summer off, the poet urges. Pick up the hickory stick again in October; in the meantime, the brighter students will have learned plenty outside the confines of the schoolroom (Martial *Epigrams* 10.62).

Avoiding Schoolwork. Students from earliest times, it seems, have sought to devise methods and excuses for their failure to be prepared in class. The poet Persius, who as a youngster was more interested in playing dice than in reading books, often smeared olive oil in his eyes before meeting with his tutor. He could then beg off the day's required recitations by claiming to be visually challenged (Persius *Satires* 3.44–51).

Classroom Management Problems. Martial also complains about his next-door neighbor the schoolmaster, who starts classes very early in the morning, in the predawn hours. This teacher tries to control his young charges by bellowing at them in a voice louder than the combined 45,000 spectators in the Coliseum could yell at a critical moment in a gladiatorial match. Martial implores the loud-mouthed schoolmaster to send his students home, at the same time wondering if his noisy neighbor would accept a fee for not teaching (Martial *Epigrams* 9.68).

Corporal Punishment. Quintilian objected to corporal punishment, even though he was well aware that the practice was established by custom and approved of by other noted teachers. Quintilian opposed such punishment for several reasons, first and foremost because it was demeaning, unnatural, and appropriate only for slaves. Second, he believed that a recalcitrant student would become even more hostile to learning after being repeatedly—or even occasionally—subjected to physical beatings. Finally, he argued that an effective teacher should have no need to resort to corporal punishment: discipline should be able to be enforced in less violent ways.

Beyond that, Quintilian saw such punishment as a poor solution to disciplinary problems. He noted that when a young student matures into adulthood, threats of bodily harm would be much more difficult to carry out, but even if administered, would have problematic results. Physical punishment can have both short- and long-term negative consequences, the worst being that children disciplined in this way could well become sullen, withdrawn, shamed, or chronically depressed.

Finally, Quintilian feared that immoral or degenerate teachers might use their right to inflict corporal punishment as a pretext for molesting innocent children. His concluding words on the subject: "I will content myself with saying that children are helpless and easily victimized, and that therefore no one should be given unlimited power over them" (Quintilian *Institutes of Oratory* 1.3.; tr. H. E. Butler LCL).

TEACHERS AND SCHOOLS

The contemporary humorist Garrison Keillor once noted that there are men among us who would not think twice about plunging into a morass of debt in order to acquire a $35,000 pickup truck, yet these same men

Teachers' Compensation

would balk at paying a music teacher a miserly hourly fee for piano lessons for their children. In the same vein, comfortably situated voters often reject school budget proposals in order to avoid having to pay an additional 25 or 50 cents per week on their property taxes. Ancient Roman parents could be equally shortsighted.

The poet Juvenal (ca. A.D. 50–ca. 127) recounts the story of a wealthy man who spent 600,000 sesterces to build private baths on his estate and even more to fund the construction of a covered colonnade, the latter being necessary so that he could go for a drive on rainy days without worrying about the mules getting wet or muddy. This spendthrift also wasted untold numbers of sesterces on a fancy banquet hall and still more on the gourmet chefs who prepared the exquisite meals served in it. Yet this man would quibble and complain about having to lay out a mere 2,000 sesterces to Quintilian, his son's teacher; "there is nothing on which [such] a father will not spend more money than on his son" (Juvenal *Satires* 7.178–188; tr. G. G. Ramsay LCL).

Juvenal also observes that teachers often have to contend with working conditions and salaries that not even a ragpicker or a blacksmith would endure. Not only that, but teachers are constantly scrutinized and criticized by parents who hold the teachers to a standard higher than any mortal could achieve:

[The teacher] must never be at fault in his grammar; he must know all history, and have all the authorities at his finger-tips. If asked a chance question . . . he must at once tell you who was the nurse of Anchises, what was the name and birthplace of Anchemolus' stepmother, to what age Acestes lived, how many flagons of Sicilian wine he presented to the Trojans. Require of him that he shall mould the young minds as a man moulds a face out of wax with his thumb; insist that he shall be a father to the whole brood, so that they shall play no nasty game, and do no nasty trick—no easy matter to watch the hands and sparkling eyes of so many youngsters! (Juvenal *Satires*, 7.230–241; tr. G. G. Ramsay LCL)

Juvenal concludes by noting that a teacher's compensation for a full year of undergoing the trials and travails of his difficult profession would equal the amount of money that a charioteer earns with just one victory on the racetrack (*Satires* 7.215–243).

The Best Teachers; the Best Schools Quintilian (*Institutes of Oratory* 2.2) set forth a number of criteria by which both teachers and schools could be judged:

1. Quintilian suggested no specific chronological age at which children should begin their formal studies under the guidance of a rhetorician.

Rather, the schooling should proceed *cum poterit*: when the young scholar can do the work.

2. The prime requisite for a teacher: *mores*, sound moral character. The ideal teacher should walk the following tightropes:

   • He must be serious, but not overly so;
   • friendly, but not a backslapper;
   • calm and restrained, but a staunch disciplinarian, as needed;
   • demanding of his students, but not too demanding;
   • he must be able to answer and ask questions, and be willing to praise his students—but not excessively;
   • correct errors, but in a manner that does not destroy a student's self-esteem.

   Furthermore, he must be able to tailor his instruction to meet the needs of individual students, and blend flexibility into the curriculum. He must be thoroughly versed in his subject matter, yet able to explain it in such a way that even a novice can learn from him. He must teach values as well as content. Perhaps above all, a good teacher must earn the respect and affection of his students.

3. Students should not give standing ovations or loudly applaud after listening to a peer's speech.

4. Boys and young men should not be thrown together in the same classes.

5. Students should be taught by the finest instructors available, even if the youngsters are more comfortable with mediocre teachers.

6. Formal schooling is preferable to home schooling.

7. Composition, composition, composition! Students should learn to write drama, fiction, and expository prose. Creativity should be encouraged.

8. Reading aloud is a worthwhile activity, especially when constructively critiqued by the teacher.

9. The best writings to be recited by a beginner? Those of Livy and Cicero.

10. Students should not be compelled to memorize their own writings.

11. Students and teachers should establish a rapport based on equal doses of respect and love.

12. *In loco parentis*. Students should regard their teachers as parents.

The Seminar Approach. Marcus Valerius Probus initially envisioned a military career for himself. But when his desired promotion to the rank of centurion never materialized, he turned instead to a life of learning and teaching. He acquired a large collection of the works of rather obscure authors and devoted himself to editing and annotating them. He did attract some students, but not many. He would meet with them individually or in small groups and discuss with them the merits and flaws of the many authors whose writings he had scrutinized (Suetonius *On Grammarians* 24).

A Demanding Acting Teacher. The noted first century B.C. actor Roscius once declared that he had never found the perfect student, one who he really thought had the potential to become a great actor. He had taught many who were good, but none who were perfect—at least according to his standards. For he believed that even the slightest flaw or defect, no matter how obscure, would stand out in an actor's performance and would overwhelm the other talents or attributes that he might bring to the stage (Cicero *On the Orator* 1.129).

Pliny Endows a School. Pliny the Younger (A.D. 62–114) relates a story about a visit he made to his northern Italian hometown of Comum. While he was there the son of one of his fellow townsmen greeted him, whereupon Pliny asked the boy if he was attending school, and where. The youngster replied in the affirmative, saying that his school was located in Mediolanum, about 25 miles from Comum. Pliny asked him why he did not go to a school in Comum, whereupon the boy's father interrupted and informed Pliny that no teachers resided in Comum—hence, no school.

Pliny was amazed that the citizens of Comum had not pooled their resources to hire teachers and thus to provide for the education of their children in their own hometown. Furthermore, he pointed out that funding for a local school could be partially offset by the money saved from the expenses that the parents incurred in sending their children to Mediolanum.

Pliny then went on to make a most generous offer to the parents of Comum: if they would raise enough money to found a school, he would contribute an additional sum, in the amount of one-third of that which they were able to provide. Pliny implied that he had both the means and the inclination to fund the entire project by himself, but he thought it important that the parents make an investment as well, so that they would be conscientious in the matter of hiring the best teachers they could find. He hoped, in fact, to stimulate a kind of reverse "brain-drain": instead of Comum's best and brightest seeking an education elsewhere, perhaps students from other towns would descend upon Comum to attend its school.

He implored his fellow citizens to consider his offer carefully, because he was very eager to see the school established. He told them that they could "do nothing better for [their] children, nothing more welcome for our town" (Pliny the Younger *Epistles* 4.13; tr. Betty Radice LCL).

Noteworthy Teachers. In his treatise entitled *De Grammaticis* (On grammarians), Suetonius provides interesting biographical data on a number of literary and rhetoric teachers who plied their pedagogical trade in ancient Rome.

Livius Andronicus and Quintus Ennius (both fl. third/second centuries B.C.) were perhaps the earliest identifiable teachers. Both offered instruction in the Greek and Latin languages, although not at a very sophisticated level. The extent of their curricula was limited to analyses of Greek works and recitations of their own Latin compositions.

The first true *grammaticus* to appear in Rome was Crates of Mallos. He happened to be visiting the city as a sort of representative of King Attalus when he fell into an open sewer on the Palatine Hill and broke his leg (ca. 169 B.C.). During his recuperation he met with numerous delegations of apologetic Romans, whom he instructed in the fine points of reading and interpreting poetry.

The formal study of literature and language flourished in the generations following Crates' entrance into Rome. Schools proliferated; by the end of the second century B.C. more than twenty had opened their doors to crowds of eager learners. Teachers saw a concomitant rise in the demand for their services. One Lucius Appuleius was paid the astounding (for a teacher) annual salary of 400,000 sesterces, provided by his patron, a wealthy Roman knight named Eficius Calvinus. At about the same time, Lutatius Daphnis, an educated teacher/slave, commanded a purchase price of 700,000 sesterces.

Grammatici also prospered outside the boundaries of Italy. Suetonius gives the names of three men who taught in Gaul (modern France): Octavius Teucer; Pescennius Iaccus, and Oppius Chares. Chares remained on the job well into his dotage, and even when blind and lame he continued to meet with his students.

The former slave Aurelius Opilius, a versatile instructor who taught philosophy, rhetoric, and grammar, was an associate of Publius Rutilius Rufus (consul in 105 B.C.). When the latter was exiled to Smyrna in 92, Opilius accompanied him; Opilius lived there to a ripe old age. His nine books on various scholarly topics corresponded to the number of Muses, whom he considered to be the protectors of writers and poets.

Marcus Antonius Gnipho, a native of Gaul, was educated in Alexandria. He enjoyed a reputation as a man of great intellect; his memory in particular was unsurpassed, and he acquired a thorough mastery of both Greek and Latin. In addition to his impressive academic credentials, he was a kind and pleasant man who never placed fee or salary demands on his students or their families—thus he received generous compensation from them, not only because of his pedagogical skills but also because of his agreeable personality and character. Gnipho taught many noted Romans, including the young Julius Caesar and the adult Cicero, even in the year in which the latter held the praetorship (66 B.C.).

Lucius Orbilius Pupillus (b. 113 B.C.), of Beneventum, was orphaned

2

Slavery

TYPES OF SLAVEOWNERS

Slavery was an economic fact of Roman life, and as such, seldom received the moral opprobrium which it would undoubtedly attract in the modern world.

A Cruel Sicilian Slaveowner

Slaves were drawn from several sources; the most important was warfare, with slavery often the fate that awaited captives. Children born to slaves inherited that servile status from their parents. Sometimes condemned criminals might be punished with hard labor, in mines and stone quarries.

Slaves might engage in various forms of employment. Often, they served as household workers performing menial tasks, but sometimes, educated slaves (always in high demand) could work as teachers or doctors. Other slaves might be put to work in private businesses, often as clerks or couriers.

Urban slaves led relatively comfortable lives. However, their counterparts in the country did not fare as well; one method of controlling urban slaves was the ever-present threat to sell them to a rancher or farm owner. Rural slaves worked long hours, under harsh working conditions.

Slaves might eventually become free (manumission), either by the initiative of the master, or through their own initiative; a slave was permitted to have a savings account of sorts (*peculium*, earned primarily through tips, wages, or gifts), and eventually might be able to purchase his freedom. Former slaves were called *liberti*, "freedmen."

In the second century B.C. there lived in the town of Enna, in Sicily, a certain Damophilus, a rich and arrogant man. This Damophilus owned large estates, many herds of cattle, and numerous slaves, whom he often treated with great cruelty. He habitually drove around the countryside in expensive carriages drawn by thoroughbred horses, all the while surrounded by a huge assemblage of servants and slaves. He lived a life of conspicuous consumption, often throwing lavish banquets at which he displayed his costly dinnerware and other dining accoutrements. He was, in sum, a rude, heartless, and uncultured man.

He used some of his excess wealth to purchase slaves, and a great number of them. Harsh treatment was the order of the day: some of them he branded like cattle; others he shackled and kept in pens like prisoners. Still others he assigned to tend his flocks and herds, but he did not provide them with even the minimum of food or clothing. On one occasion a group of his household slaves appeared stark naked before him and begged for some clothes. Damophilus eyed them angrily and suggested that they go out to the public road and plead for garments from travelers. After dispensing that bit of advice he ordered that they be tied to pillars, beaten savagely, and then sent back to their work stations or their cages.

This cruel master mistreated his slaves continually, sometimes for no reason whatsoever. And his wife, Metallis, was no better. She dished out punishments to her servants, as well as any other slaves she might come across, that equaled the abuse that her husband customarily laid upon them. Eventually the slaves could no longer take it. They began to plot ways to assassinate Damophilus and Metallis; they were not worried at all about the possibility of failure. They had long since decided that any fate would be easier to bear than life under their two masters. So they approached a slave who lived nearby, a man named Eunus.

Eunus hailed from Syria, and he brought with him to Sicily from the east some mysterious powers. He was a magician and a fortuneteller. He claimed to have a direct pipeline to the gods, who (he said) appeared to him at night in dreams, or sometimes even in broad daylight, and informed him of future events. This information he passed along to unwitting audiences, and in great profusion. Many times his predictions turned out to be false, but he was right just often enough to maintain his credibility and even enhance his prophetic reputation.

He devised a way whereby he could spit flames from his mouth. He would obtain an empty nutshell, bore holes at each end, stuff fuel and burning embers into it, and place the whole thing into his mouth. Then, at precisely the most dramatic moment, he would blow on the nutshell, thus fanning the embers and producing a flame, which gave the appearance that he breathed fire.

Eunus once claimed that the Syrian goddess Atargatis had materialized before his eyes to inform him that he would one day be a king. Eunus told this story not only to his fellow slaves but also to his master, Antigenes. Most people who heard the tale did not believe it, Antigenes among them. But he humored the man who would be king; he even introduced him at banquets and interrogated him in front of the guests, asking him how he would behave toward Sicily's landed gentry if ever he did indeed don the crown and purple robe.

Eunus gave all the right answers, saying that he would treat all his conjectural subjects with kind consideration. So entertaining was he, and so clever at embellishing his yarns, that the laughing diners customarily presented him with table scraps, at the same time admonishing him to remember their benefactions when he ascended to the throne.

This Eunus was the man to whom the slaves of Damophilus made their appeal.

Eunus played to his audience. In mysterious-sounding tones he told them that the gods had favored their enterprise, and he urged them to put the plan in motion immediately. The slaves agreed; they quickly mustered 400 men, who armed themselves as best they could, and marched upon Enna, with Eunus as their leader. (He used his fire-breathing trick during the assault to increase the ardor of his followers.)

The slave-army showed no mercy. They killed babies before the eyes of the mothers and then raped the mothers in the presence of their help-less husbands. When Eunus and the 400 discovered that Damophilus and Metallis were in a nearby park, a small detachment of the army was sent to fetch them into the city. This was no sooner ordered than done, and before long the two were standing captive, in the town theater, in front of their (now) former slaves.

Damophilus began to beg for mercy and was actually winning over some in the crowd; however, two of the men who hated him the most deeply, Hermeias and Zeuxis, were not swayed by his words. Fearing that Damophilus might escape punishment through his oratory, they drew their weapons and slew him.

Immediately the 400 helped one of Eunus's many prophecies come true: they named him king. And not because of any regal bearing or administrative skill, but simply because of his sideshow appeal and also his name, which in Greek means "friendly." Eunus's first royal act was to decree that all the surviving citizens of Enna be executed, except for weaponry mongers, whom he placed in chains and ordered to fabricate additional arms. He also spared the men who had indulged him at the banquets (mentioned previously). He ordered these men to be whisked away from Enna and set free. They were amazed at their good fortune, that their condescension at the dinners would be repaid with such an act of mercy.

Metallis was turned over to her former slaves to do with as they wished. Their wish: to hurl her over a cliff, but only after torturing her first.

Damophilus and Metallis had a daughter, a young girl noted for her gentle nature and generous spirit. She had always taken pity on the slaves who suffered physical abuse at the hands of her parents, and she had showed compassion for those who were bound or caged. Because of these past acts of kindness, none of the slaves dared to harm her. Several of their number were chosen to convey the girl safely to the town of Catana, where some of her close relatives lived.

Not surprisingly, the Roman authorities soon took note of the events in Sicily and dispatched a military force to deal with the situation. As the Romans approached the town of Enna, it did not require any special prophetic powers for Eunus to perceive that his life was in danger. So he fled to the nearby hills, taking with him a contingent of 1,000 men. The Romans pursued them; many of the 1,000 killed themselves or each other prior to the arrival of the legions. But Eunus, along with a cook, a baker, a masseuse, and a jester, hid in a cave. Unfortunately, the cave offered no protection: the five were discovered, dragged out, and sent to prison, where Eunus soon died.

Diodorus Siculus, the source for the details of Eunus's life and times, summarizes the incident well: "Even among slaves, human nature needs no instructor in regard to just repayment, whether of gratitude or of revenge" (Diodorus Siculus, *Library of History*, 34/35. 2ff; tr. Francis R. Walton).

A Kind and Generous Master   Mark Antony's (82–30 B.C.) father, Marcus Antonius Creticus, was a rather inept politician and soldier, but in his private life he had a reputation for kindness and generosity. His inability to deny loans and other indulgences to his friends caused his wife to closely monitor his activities, especially because the family coffers were not overflowing with sesterces.

One day, a friend in need approached Creticus; because at that time he had no money to lend, he hit upon this scheme: he ordered a slave to fill a silver bowl with water and bring it to him in the presence of his friend. Creticus then slapped some of the water onto his face, as if preparing to shave, while simultaneously ordering the slave to leave on a bogus errand. As soon as the two men were alone, Creticus dumped the water out of the bowl and gave it to his friend with instructions to sell it and keep the proceeds. This he did.

Unfortunately, Creticus's wife (not knowing about the transaction) soon missed the bowl and initiated a thorough search for it. When it did not turn up, she proposed torturing the household slaves one at a time until the guilty party confessed (for she was certain that a slave had stolen it).

At this point her husband intervened and told her the truth. He begged and pleaded for forgiveness, which after a time he succeeded in gaining from her. And so no slaves were put to the test (Plutarch *Life of Mark Antony* 1).

SLAVES AND FREEDMEN

A prudent and humane householder need not necessarily seek friends exclusively in the forum or in the halls of government buildings; for if he behaves courteously to his own slaves, he may find among them some true friends. Slaves are not naturally hostile to their masters; they only become that way if the master treats them with cruelty. Conversely, slaves who receive kind treatment often reward that kindness in unexpected ways.

Urbinus, a member of the Roman nobility, had for some unknown reason been placed on a list of persons to be executed. Upon hearing of his likely fate, he immediately hurried from Rome to his estate at Reate, where a hideout was prepared for him.

Unfortunately, the precise location of his hiding place was revealed to the authorities whose task it was to execute him. Fortunately, before they arrived at Reate to carry out their grim mission, one of his slaves donned Urbinus's clothing and signet ring in an effort to masquerade as Urbinus. The trick worked; the assassins mistakenly killed the loyal slave.

Afterwards, Urbinus was pardoned. Out of gratitude he ordered an inscribed monument to be built to commemorate his slave's selfless action (Macrobius *Saturnalia* 1.2).

Aesopus, a freedman of Demosthenes during the time of the emperor Augustus, had been engaging in illicit behavior with Julia, the emperor's daughter. As a way to obtain evidence against Demosthenes, Aesopus was tortured. But the stoical freedman was the picture of steadfastness and would say nothing to incriminate his former master. Finally other witnesses came forward to testify against Demosthenes, and the faithful Aesopus was released.

Sometimes even cruel masters were repaid not in coin but with consideration. For example, Antius Restio learned that his name had found its way onto a proscription list, so naturally he fled from his home. Most of his slaves jumped at the chance to help themselves to the possessions that Restio left behind in his haste to flee. But one, who had been shackled and branded at Restio's demand, but later freed by a merciful stranger, pursued his master—not to take vengeance but to encourage him, help him find a place to hide, and care for him. For the slave believed that it was fate, and not any human agency, that was responsible for his mistreatment of earlier days.

Later, when the slave observed that the pursuing authorities were nearby, he killed an old man whom he happened to meet, built a funeral pyre, set it ablaze, and threw the corpse onto the fire. He then ran to the pursuers and told them that he had slain his cruel master. The story made sense to them, and they saw no reason to disbelieve him, especially with the burning fire as evidence. So they departed, and Restio survived (Macrobius *Saturnalia* 1.2).

Sometimes slaves were not only loyal and brave in protecting their masters, but also ingenious. When the town of Grumentum was under attack, some of the slaves of a certain lady who lived in the town deserted her and joined the attackers. After Grumentum was captured, these same slaves assaulted their former place of residence and dragged their mistress into the streets. They gave every indication of preparing to have their wicked ways with her, all the while loudly shouting that the treatment she was about to receive was exactly what she deserved. But once they had transported her out of Grumentum and well away from the town's attackers, their behavior changed. They showed the highest respect and loyalty to her and offered her their protection (Macrobius *Saturnalia* 1.2).

Publius Cornelius Scipio (d. 211 B.C.), father of the renowned Africanus, also owed his life to a loyal slave. During a battle against Hannibal's forces, Scipio was severely wounded. His men left him to die, but a slave who happened to be present hoisted Scipio onto a horse and led him through the chaos and mayhem to safety (Macrobius *Saturnalia* 1.2).

Slaves were generally not eligible for service in the Roman army, but even this prohibition was waived on occasion. After the Battle of Cannae in 216 B.C., for example, 8,000 able-bodied slaves were enlisted, even though it would have been less costly to ransom the soldiers who had been captured by the Carthaginians (Macrobius *Saturnalia* 1.2).

How Many Slaves Does It Take to Maintain a Farm? Cato the Elder (*On Agriculture* 10–11) suggests the following personnel requirements for a 150-acre orchard:

Thirteen workers:

one overseer

one housekeeper

five general farmhands

three plowmen

one mule driver

one swineherd

one shepherd

For a sixty-acre vineyard, Cato specifies sixteen workers:

one overseer

one housekeeper

ten general farmhands

one plowman

one mule driver

one willow worker

one swineherd

In his book on agriculture, Varro adds that Saserna, an authority on things cultivated, asserts that one man should be able to maintain a 5-acre plot and that he ought to be able to plow it over in 45 days. However, an industrious farmer, working solo, should be able to cultivate nearly 1 acre in 4 days or the entire amount (5 acres) in about 32 days. However, 13 days of leeway need to be added to the mix to account for inclement weather, sickness, or vacation time (Varro *On Agriculture* 1.18).

A former slave from Assisi by the name of Publius De-cimius Eros Merula certainly did well for himself. He carved out a multifaceted career in medicine and optom-etry and also dabbled in politics as a member of the town **From Slavery to Surgery** council. (His membership, however, did not come without a price: 2,000 sesterces, to be exact.)

He paid 50,000 sesterces for his freedom and made several benefactions to the community, including 37,000 sesterces for statues in a temple of Hercules and 30,000 for road paving (*CIL* 11.5400).

TWO EXTREME INCIDENTS INVOLVING SLAVES

Pedanius Secundus, a city prefect, was murdered in A.D. 61 by one of his own slaves. The motive for the dastardly deed was variously ascribed to a dis- **Pedanius Secundus** agreement over the terms of the slave's manumission or his rivalry with his master in a love triangle.

The perpetrator was apprehended and convicted; according to Roman law and custom, not only he but the entire household of some 400 slaves were condemned to death. The prospect of an indiscriminate slaughter of so many innocent people provoked a riot in the city, and ultimately the Roman senate was compelled to deal with the matter. Some senators agreed with the popular sentiment, but many more favored upholding the letter of the law, no matter how bloodied it might become. One of these law-and-order types was a senator named Gaius Cassius. His arguments were as follows.

He began by stating that during previous senatorial debates on points of law he generally had said nothing so as not to appear unduly pompous, even though he had a better grasp of the issues than did the debaters. But in this case he felt it was high time for him to be heard. He referred to the law passed a few years earlier (in 57) specifying punishment for all slaves in a household if even only one were found guilty of assassinating the master, let alone a city prefect. To exonerate the 400 would be tantamount to a declaration of justifiable homicide, he argued.

He claimed that the law of 57 was a sound and prudent piece of legislation, necessary for the protection of the established order. And if innocent people occasionally died as a result of applying the law, so be it. Who ever said that life was fair? With this sentiment, he concluded his remarks.

No senator opposed him, but an angry crowd with other ideas remained outside the senate house. Those in the assemblage were outraged that so many blameless people—including the very young and the very old—would be dragged to their deaths. In the end the executions were carried out, but not until the emperor Claudius called out contingents of soldiers to keep the mob from interfering (Tacitus *Annals* 14.42–45).

Publius Vedius Pollio
Publius Vedius Pollio, a first century B.C. Roman knight, had great wealth but also an unsavory cruel streak. One day he was entertaining at his home no less a personage than Augustus himself. When one of the household slaves accidentally dropped a crystal goblet, causing it to shatter, the infuriated Pollio ordered the unfortunate slave to be tossed into a fish pond. This was not a severe penalty, except that the pond was stocked with voracious, man-eating lampreys.

The butter-fingered slave somehow slipped from the grasp of the executioners and fled to Augustus's feet, where he begged not to be set free but only to be executed in a more humane fashion. Disgusted by the cruelty of the proposed punishment, Augustus not only pardoned the slave on the spot but also ordered that all of Pollio's crystal dinnerware meet the pavement in the same way as the first cup and that the lamprey-infested pond be drained and filled in (Seneca *On Anger* 3.40).

LEGALLY FREE, BUT A SLAVE NONETHELESS

Cicero noted the following ways in which a free citizen may nonetheless, in some respects, be a slave:

1. If slavery can be defined or characterized by a person's lack of free will, then anyone who is saddled with a greedy, violent, or simple-minded nature could be considered a slave.

2. A man who is under the thumb of a woman, who is constantly at her beck and call, could hardly be called free. "She asks, he must give; she calls, he must come; she throws him out, he must go; she threatens, he must tremble." Cicero claims that this is one of the lowest forms of slavery, even if the "slave" is a member of Rome's noblest family.

3. People who devote inordinate amounts of time and effort to admiring and acquiring works of art could be considered slaves of the very things that they aspire to control through ownership.

4. Those who would do almost anything for money—no matter how demeaning—could be equated to slaves. The prime example: a legacy-hunter who continually flatters and waits upon a wealthy old widower or dowager in the hopes of a big payoff when the old person dies and the will is read.

5. An excessive ambition for political office, military command, or provincial governorship can turn a free man into a slave, if he is willing to sell out his honor to satisfy that ambition.

6. Even if a man has become a consul or a governor, and even if he has attained great wealth, and amassed a huge art collection, and married a compatible wife, and has not given in to a violent or avaricious nature, and has found satisfaction in all these fulfilled life goals, he could still be a slave, if in thrall to the fear caused by a guilty conscience.

   Even the most powerful man in the Roman government would be a slave if reason and truth have failed to set him free.

(Cicero *Paradoxes of the Stoics* 33–41; tr. H. Rackham LCL)

REFERENCES

Cicero: *Paradoxes of the Stoics*.
CIL 11.5400.
Diodorus Siculus: *Library of History*.
Macrobius: *Saturnalia*.
Plutarch: *Life of Mark Antony*.
Seneca: *On Anger*.
Tacitus: *Annals*.
Varro: *On Agriculture*.

3

Food and Dining

THE ANCIENT ROMANS AT THE DINNER TABLE

Contrary to the sometimes prevailing modern view, most ancient Romans did not customarily gorge themselves at lavish dinner parties or engage in cycles of eating and vomiting and then eating still more. A majority of Romans undoubtedly were restrained in their eating habits, a condition perhaps dictated as much by economics as by appetites.

The basic food groups were grains and vegetables; various kinds of bread and porridge were produced from the former. Vegetables included beans, peas, onions, radishes, lettuce, cabbage, celery, and cucumbers. Fruits also formed a part of the typical Roman's diet; figs, grapes, apples, and pears were staples. Eggs, cheese, mushrooms, and olive oil were also important food items, and spices, especially salt and herbs, were widely used and enjoyed.

Meat was generally too expensive for most household budgets to afford on a regular basis; pork and veal were the two most readily available meat products. Fish and poultry were probably more commonly eaten than animal meats.

Without doubt, the "national drink" of the Romans was wine. Usually mixed with water and honey, it was served even to young children. Milk and beer were also available but were less popular than wine.

The ancient Romans, like their modern counterparts, consumed three meals per day. Breakfast (*jentaculum*) was a light meal, consisting perhaps of bread, cheese, and fruit; lunch (*prandium*), eaten around noon, might feature bread, eggs, vegetables, and perhaps fish. Supper (*cena*) was the day's main meal. It generally included three courses: appetizers (*gustatio*); the often multi-course *cena* itself; and dessert (*mensae secundae*). In wealthy Roman homes, meals were eaten in the *triclinium*, a dining room equipped with three couches for reclining as well as a dinner table.

Food requiring cooking was usually boiled or roasted, and most homes had ovens, or small, hibachi-like braziers suitable for the purpose. Bread was baked in home ovens or bought from commercial bakeries.

Alternatively, if one's hectic daily schedule precluded time for meal preparation, eating out was always an option. The restaurant and tavern trade flourished throughout Italy, although the patronizing of such establishments was viewed with some disapproval by upper-class Romans. Some of the restaurants were of the "fast food" variety, where a customer could eat in or purchase a meal "to go." Some were even designed in such a way that customers could obtain meals without leaving their wagons or entering the restaurant at all, the prototype of "drive-through" service.

Healthy Eating The physician Celsus (fl. first century A.D.) recommends the following foods and drink as beneficial to the stomach: harsh, sour, and moderately salted foods; unleavened bread: soaked rice or barley; roasted or boiled birds; beef and other kinds of meat, as long as lean (rather than fatty) cuts are consumed; pig parts, including feet, ears, and womb; lettuce; cooked gourds; cherries, mulberries, pears, apples, pomegranates, preserved raisins; dates, soft eggs, preserved white olives, tree-ripened black olives; dry wine; oysters, snails, fish. Very hot or very cold foods and drinks are recommended.

Included on Celsus's list of stomach-unfriendly food and drink are the following: lukewarm consumables and anything that is too salty, excessively sweet, stewed, and especially fatty; leavened bread or barley bread; herbs soaked in fish sauce or olive oil; honey; raisin wine; dairy products, including milk and all kinds of cheeses; grapes; figs; and certain spices or seasonings, such as thyme, catnip, mint, or sorrel juice (Celsus *On Medicine* 2. 24–25).

A Special Dinner Menu A first century B.C. list of foods served at the inauguration of priests survives. The first course consisted of sea-urchins, plain oysters, two sorts of mussels, a thrush on asparagus, a fatted hen, a ragout of oysters and mussels, black and white chestnuts; then different kinds of shellfish and marine animals with becaficos, loins of does and wild boars, game-pie, and purple fish with becaficos. The chief course consisted of udders of sows, a pig's head, fricassee of fish and sow's udder, two kinds of duck (boiled or otherwise prepared), hares, roasted game, a meal pudding and Picentine bread. The menu of the dessert is lost (list quoted from Friedlaender *Roman Life and Manners* 2.149).

The antiquarian Marcus Terentius Varro (116–27 B.C.) once made a list of districts that produced the best of certain kinds of food and drink. His list included:

Food/Drink	Best Place to Get It/Them
Corn	Campania
Wine	Falernus
Oil	Casinum
Figs	Tusculum
Honey	Tarentum
Fish	Tiber River

(Varro *Antiquities of Man*, quoted in Macrobius *Saturnalia* 3.16).

DINING WITH THE ELITE ROMANS

One of ancient Rome's most famous gourmands was Lucius Licinius Lucullus (ca. 117–56 B.C.). After his long and distinguished public career, he enjoyed a retirement of ease and leisure. This was especially true when it came to dinners and their trimmings.

A typical Lucullan bash featured expensively dyed tablecloths and pitchers studded with gemstones; live entertainment, usually actors who would perform poetic recitations or excerpts of plays; and every kind of meat dish imaginable, as well as exquisitely prepared side dishes.

A story once circulated about Pompey the Great (106–48 B.C.) who, when ill, was advised by his physicians to eat a thrush. Pompey's servants replied that thrushes were nowhere to be found in that season of the year (winter), except on Lucullus's estates, where he raised them. Pompey refused to indebt himself to Lucullus through the procurement of a thrush, instead ordering the servants to concoct some equivalent medicinal preparation.

Lucullus thoroughly enjoyed his luxurious lifestyle and never seemed to care if others criticized or envied him. He once entertained some Greek visitors for several days, but as the costly amenities continued to flow forth, the guests became increasingly uncomfortable. Finally, they told him, they could stay no longer, because Lucullus was running up such a large tab on their account. Lucullus smiled and replied that although some of his expenditures were on their account, most of the outlays were on his account.

On another occasion he was scheduled to eat dinner alone. His cooks, knowing this, prepared a modest meal for him, with only one course. When the unadorned food was placed before him. Lucullus was furious and demanded to speak to the servant responsible for such slim pickings. The servant's explanation: because he knew that Lucullus would be dining without guests, he thought that a less costly meal would suffice. "What are you talking about?" bellowed Lucullus. "Don't you know that Lucullus is feeding Lucullus today?"

Lucullus's residences featured a number of dining rooms, each with its own serving staff, cookware, table settings, and budget. Therefore it was relatively easy for him to organize a lavish dinner party on short notice. One day Cicero and Pompey approached him while he was relaxing in the forum; they said that they wished to discuss some business with him over dinner. To this request he readily assented and invited them to do so at his home, but in a day or two. They protested that the matter was pressing and could not be postponed even for that long; they were hoping to embarrass Lucullus into serving them ordinary food in an unpretentious setting, as there would not be enough time for him to arrange an expensive spread.

But Lucullus got the last laugh by ordering his servants to immediately set three places at the Apollo, the name he gave to one of his most elegant dining rooms; dinners there regularly incurred great expense. So when Pompey and Cicero were ushered into the Apollo, they were astonished, both at the costliness of the meal and at the speed with which their host was able to assemble it (Plutarch *Life of Lucullus* 41).

Menu Items for the Elite

Lampreys. The lamprey was judged to be a desirable dinner delicacy by many of the elite in Rome, as Macrobius indicates in the following anecdotes.

Lucius Licinius Crassus, an early first century B.C. orator, was held in the highest esteem by his contemporaries; he eventually rose to the office of censor. And yet, when a prized lamprey of his died in the fish pond on the grounds of his estate, he donned mourning garb as if a member of his own family had passed away. This incident quickly became grist for Rome's rumor mill, to the point that his colleague in the censorship, Gnaeus Domitius, made a speech in the senate criticizing him for such ridiculous and inappropriate behavior. Crassus rose to his feet to respond. He admitted that he had mourned the loss of the lamprey, but he also claimed that his action was entirely fitting.

Cato the Younger (95–46 B.C.) inherited a fish pond from another noted first century B.C. lover of fine living, Lucius Licinius Lucullus. Because Cato had no use for the lampreys with which the pond was stocked, he sold them all for a sum of 40,000 sesterces. The incident, says Macrobius, illustrates how men of wealth—like Lucullus, the orator Hortensius, and others—valued the lamprey as a gourmand's delight.

Lampreys were imported to Rome from Sicilian waters, where they were called "floaters." They received this name because they habitually swam near the water's surface. They were unable to dive because of their prolonged exposure to the hot summer sun and also because of their plumpness, which added to their buoyancy. Fishermen found it an easy task to simply "harvest" the lampreys by grabbing them with their hands and tossing them into the fishing boats.

Lampreys were relatively common in Rome, at least in the fish ponds and dining rooms of the city's wealthier inhabitants. But even average citizens could occasionally feast on the creatures; when Julius Caesar, for example, was celebrating one of his many military triumphs, he purchased for the people 6,000 pounds of lampreys from a certain Gavius Hirrius. This Hirrius, although not inordinately affluent, was able to sell his country estate for 4,000,000 sesterces, its primary selling point being the well-stocked fish ponds (Macrobius *Saturnalia* 15.3–9).

Sturgeon. Alongside the lamprey on the list of luxurious menu selections was the sturgeon.

Cicero (106–43 B.C.) confirms the sturgeon's lofty status in his philosophical essay *On Fate* (as recorded by Macrobius) in which he relates an anecdote about Scipio Aemilianus. One evening, when Scipio and his friend Pontius were relaxing at Scipio's home in Lavernium, a large sturgeon was served to him. Pleased that such a rare delicacy was to be consumed at the evening meal, he was about to invite several more friends to join him. But Pontius cautioned him against such liberality, pointing out that it was not often that sturgeon was on the menu and that he ought to be selective about who, and how many, could share in the repast (Macrobius *Saturnalia* 3.16).

By Pliny the Younger's time (late first, early second century A.D.) the sturgeon had for some unknown reason fallen into disfavor among gourmands. But it experienced a renaissance in the following century, at which time contemporary authors noted that "the fish [had in former times been] brought to table by servants crowned with garlands and to the accompaniment of the flute" (Macrobius *Saturnalia* 3.16; tr. P. V. Davies).

Boar's Meat. In Rome's earlier days, boar's meat was considered a disgusting consumable; during his censorship in 184 B.C., for example, Cato the Elder delivered several speeches condemning the practice of eating such a food.

Tastes, however, changed. In the first century B.C., Publius Servilius Rullus became the first man on Roman record to cook and serve a whole boar at his dinner parties. By the first century A.D. it was not unusual for two or even three boars to be served at banquets (Pliny the Elder *Natural History* 8.210).

Wrasse. The wrasse (a kind of fish that according to Webster's *Third International Dictionary* is an "elongate compressed but heavy-bodied usu[ally] brilliantly colored marine fish . . . related to the parrot fishes, but hav[ing] separate teeth in their jaws and conspicuous thick lips") was so rare in the seas around Italy that there was not even a Latin word for it. However, a certain Optatus, who as a naval commander had sailed far and wide, learned of the wrasse and caught and sent home a great quantity of them (alive); ships with specially designed tanks were used to accomplish this task. The fish were released into the coastal waters of Italy, "sown in the sea as grain is sown in the earth," as Macrobius put it.

Furthermore, Optatus suggested that for the five-year period following the wrasse-stocking program, any fisherman who caught one should immediately return it to its watery adoptive home (Macrobius *Saturnalia* 3.16; tr. P. V. Davies).

Pearls. Pliny the Elder (A.D. 23–79) records a strange menu selection of Clodius, son of the actor Aesopus. This Clodius was evidently fairly wealthy, having inherited a large estate from his father. One day he developed an odd hankering to know how pearls might taste. To find out, he did the obvious thing: he popped one into his mouth! Satisfied that pearls were indeed tasty, he decided to serve some at the next banquet he put on. He gave his guests one pearl apiece to eat so that they, too, might share in the pearl's palate-pleasing characteristics (Pliny the Elder *Natural History* 9.122).

Mark Antony (82–30 B.C.), whose reputation for excessive drinking and eating was well established in Rome, once actually proposed a law limiting expenditures on banquets. The circumstances that led to this proposal were as follows:

Cleopatra had made a "friendly wager" with him that she could fund a dinner party costing 10,000,000 sesterces, a sum greater than even he— the exemplar of extravagance, the king of costliness, the lord of lavishness—had ever spent on such a party. Antony could not believe that she would be able to pull it off, so he accepted her wager, with Munatius Plancus holding the money and playing the role of impartial arbiter.

The next day Cleopatra put on a spread—elegant and expensive but not outlandishly so, by Antonian standards, at least—so he began to feel confident of winning the bet. But then Cleopatra ordered one of the servants to bring out a drinking glass, which she filled with vinegar; in one swift motion she removed a large pearl from one of her earrings and dropped it into the glass. The vinegar dissolved the pearl; Cleopatra downed the pearly drink and was ready to declare herself the winner, because the pearl she had swallowed was by itself worth 10,000,000 sesterces. However, before claiming her winnings she raised her hand and was preparing to consume the valuable pearl in her other earring in the same way, when Plancus intervened and officially ruled that Antony had lost the bet. After falling victim to Cleopatra's trickery, Antony apparently was motivated to propose his sumptuary law.

The remaining pearl survived the ordeal. Later (after the Battle of Actium in 31 B.C.) it was taken from Cleopatra and brought to Rome. Its immensity could be illustrated by the fact that it was cut in half and a "new" pearl was fashioned from each half; the two "new" pearls were still considered large enough to be worthy of a place on the statue of Venus in the Pantheon (Macrobius *Saturnalia*).

From time to time Roman politicians proposed, and Roman legislatures passed, mostly unenforceable **Sumptuary Laws** sumptuary laws designed to regulate the amount of money that could be spent on banquets and the kinds of foods served at them. These policies sometimes ushered in unexpected consequences, as the following Ciceronian letter shows:

In case you [Marcus Fadius Gallus] should wonder what caused this attack [of diarrhea] or how I brought it upon myself, it was that sumptuary law, which is supposed to have inaugurated "plain living,"—it was that, I say, which proved my undoing. For your gourmets, in their anxiety to bring into favor the fruits of the earth, which are exempted under that law, season their mushrooms, potherbs, and greens of every kind with a skill that makes them irresistibly delicious. I was let in for that sort of food at an augural banquet at Lentulus's house [to celebrate Lentulus's selection as an augur], with the result that I was seized with an attack of diarrhea so persistent that not until today has it shown any signs of stopping. So I, who had no difficulty abstaining from oysters and lampreys, was [done in by beets and mallow]. So for the future I should take better care of myself. . . . I intend staying on here until I am restored to health, for I have lost both strength and weight. But once I have beaten off this attack, I shall easily, I hope, recover both. (Cicero *Letters to His Friends* 7.26; tr. W. Glynn Williams LCL)

For an example that provided the impetus for sumptuary laws, one might cite the 8,000-sesterce mullet. During the reign of the emperor Caligula (A.D. 37–41), a certain Asinius Celer paid that very sum for a mullet and dared his fellow gourmands to top that price. The recorder of this anecdote, Pliny the Elder, goes on to remark that a skilled cook once fetched a higher purchase price than a horse, but that now "the price of three horses is given for a cook, and the price of three cooks for a fish" (Pliny the Elder *Natural History* 9.67).

Plutarch (ca. A.D. 50–ca. 120) relates an anecdote told to his grandfather by a certain Philotas, a young medical student living in Alexandria at the time in which Mark Antony was courting Cleopatra. Philotas developed a friendship with one of Cleopatra's cooks, who invited him to take a tour of the royal kitchen on a day on which a feast was being prepared for Antony and Cleopatra. Philotas was flabbergasted at the sights that met his eyes: a huge abundance of food, including no fewer than eight wild boars, all in various stages of preparation.

A Feast for Antony and Cleopatra

Philotas figured that there must be a virtual army of guests expected, but the cook laughingly explained that only about twelve diners would partake of the meal. But they were extremely demanding diners, and every course had to be done to a turn—and at the exact time that they desired. Unfortunately, the kitchen staff never knew precisely when that demand would come; sometimes Antony wanted to eat immediately, but at other times, only after drinking some wine and chatting with his fellow diners. Therefore, said the cook, "not one, but many suppers are arranged; for the precise time is hard to hit" (Plutarch *Life of Mark Antony* 28; tr. B. Perrin LCL).

Dinner with the Emperor Augustus The emperor Augustus (ruled 27 B.C.–A.D. 14) was not the most gregarious of men, but nevertheless he enjoyed giving formal banquets, as Suetonius relates:

He gave dinner parties constantly and always formally, with great regard to the rank and personality of his guests. Valerius Messala writes that he never invited a freedman to dinner with the exception of Menas, and then only when he had been enrolled among the freeborn after betraying the fleet of Sextus Pompey. . . . He would sometimes come to table late . . . and leave early, allowing his guests to begin to dine before he took his place and keep their places after he went out. He served a dinner of three courses or of six when he was most lavish, without needless extravagance but with the greatest goodfellowship. For he drew into general conversation those who were silent or chatted under their breath, and introduced music and actors, or even strolling players from the circus, and especially story-tellers.

Augustus's own eating habits were anything but luxurious. He did not eat much, and when he did eat, ordinary fare was usually the order of the day; he particularly liked bread, fish, cheese, and figs. Sometimes he ate "on the road" when traveling in a carriage; on these occasions a little bread, a few grapes, and maybe some dates would be on the menu. He drank wine, but only in very moderate amounts and almost never before dinner.

Because he often ate in between meals—favoring bread, cucumber slices, lettuce, or apples on these occasions—he might not eat anything at all at his formal dinner parties (Suetonius *Life of Augustus* 74, 76, 77; tr. J. C. Rolfe LCL).

The Ultimate Bash Perhaps the most famous Roman dinner party ever was the one thrown by Petronius's (d. A.D. 66) fictional freedman, Trimalchio, the protagonist in Detronius's "Trimalchio's Dinner," a chapter in *Satyricon.*

Gustatio (part I): White and black olives; hot sausages; plums and pomegranate seeds (31).

Gustatio (part II): Peahen's eggs, stuffed with cooked sparrow and served with spiced egg yolk (33).

Gustatio (part III): A large round plate with engraved images of the twelve signs of the zodiac, and appropriate foods placed under each sign, thus (35):

Sign	Food/decoration
Aries	Chickpea
Taurus	Slice of beef
Gemini	Kidneys
Cancer	Flowers
Leo	African fig
Virgo	Barren sow's paunch
Libra	A set of balances, with a muffin on one side, and a cake on the other
Scorpio	A small fish
Sagittarius	The fish called an oblade
Capricorn	Crawfish
Aquarius	Goose
Pisces	Two mullets

Cena (first course): Various kinds of fowl; sow's bellies; a rabbit prepared with wings, to resemble Pegasus; fish served in a special sauce (36).

Cena (second course): Wild boar (whole), with a basket hanging from each tusk: one of these was filled with dried dates, the other, fresh dates; placed around the boar were small cakes in the form of suckling piglets, to show that the boar was a female (40).

Cena (third course): Three white pigs were led into the dining room, whereupon Trimalchio asked his guests to select one of them, and that one would be butchered and cooked immediately (48). In a short time—too short, it seemed—the cooked pig was brought before the guests. Upon examining it, however, Trimalchio noticed that it had not been properly gutted. He demanded that the forgetful cook appear immediately to explain such an unforgivable omission. The cook came out, but Trimalchio—at the urging of his guests—did not order the man to be beaten, but instead to finish gutting the pig right then and there. And as the cook carved away, precooked sausages and puddings poured out of the pig (49).

Secundae mensae: Cakes and various kinds of grapes and other fruits; pastries in the shape of small birds, filled with raisins and nuts; oysters, scallops, and snails (60, 69, 70).

One of the guests, the late-arriving Habinnas, had already been to a dinner party that evening. He describes for Trimalchio the fare he had already consumed:

First we had a pig crowned with a wine-cup, garnished with honey cakes, and giblets very well done, and beetroot, of course, and pure wholemeal bread, which I prefer to white myself. . . . The next dish was a cold tart, with excellent Spanish wine poured over warm honey. Indeed I ate a lot of the tart and gave myself such a soaking of honey . . . A choice of nuts and an apple each. I took two myself, and I have got them here tied up in my napkin. . . . There was a piece of bear in view. . . . I ate over a pound myself, for it tasted like proper wild boar. What I say is this, since bears eat up us poor men, how much better right has a poor man to eat up a bear? To finish up with we had cheese mellowed in new wine, and snails all around, and pieces of tripe, and liver in little dishes, and eggs in caps, and turnip, and mustard. . . . Pickled olives were brought round in a dish, too, and some greedy creatures took three fistfuls. (Petronius *Satyricon* 66; tr. W.H.D. Rouse LCL)

RECIPES

Note: Numbers appearing after the recipe titles indicate book and recipe number from Apicius's *De Re Coquinaria* (On cooking). All translations are by Joseph Vehling and are quoted from the 1977 Dover edition, which is a republication of the original version (Chicago: Walter M. Hill, 1936).

Honey Refresher for Travelers (1.2)

The wayfarer's honey refresher (so called because it gives endurance and strength to pedestrians).

[The traveler's honey refresher] is made in this manner: Flavor honey with ground pepper and skim; in the moment of serving, put honey in a cup, as much as is desired to obtain the right degree of sweetness, and mix with wine, not more than a needed quantity; also, add some wine to the spiced honey to facilitate its flow and the mixing.

Fine Ragout of Brains and Bacon (4.148)

The dish of bacon and brains is made in this manner: Strain hard-boiled eggs with parboiled brains [calf's or pig's], the skin and the nerves of which have been removed. Also, cook chicken giblets, all in proportion to the fish. Put this aforesaid mixture in a saucepan, placed the cooked bacon in the center, grind pepper and lovage [herbs]. And to sweeten, add a dash of mead. Heat. When hot, stir briskly with a rue whip, and bind [thicken] with roux [flour].

Peas (Supreme Style) (5.186)

Cook the peas with oil and a piece of sow's belly. Put in a saucepan: broth, leek heads, green coriander, and put on the fire to be cooked. Dice tid-bits [finely chopped meats]. Similarly cook thrushes or other small game birds, or take sliced chicken or diced brain, properly cooked.

Further cook, in the available broth, Lucanian sausage and bacon; cook leeks in water. Crush a pint of toasted pignolia nuts; also crush pepper, lovage [herbs], origany [herbs], and ginger. Dilute with the broth of pork.

Take a square baking dish, suitable for turning over; oil [it] well. Sprinkle [on the bottom] a layer of crushed nuts, upon which put some peas, fully covering the bottom of the dish. On top of this, arrange slices of the bacon, leeks, and sliced Lucanian sausage. Again cover with a layer of peas, and alternate all the rest of the available edibles in the manner described, until the dish is filled, concluding at last with a layer of peas.

Bake this dish in the oven, or put it into a slow fire, so that it may be baked thoroughly. [Next, make a sauce of the following]: Put yolks of hard-boiled eggs in the mortar with white pepper, nuts, honey, white wine, and a little broth. Mix and put it into a saucepan to be cooked. When done, turn out the peas into a large [dish], and mask them with this sauce, which is called white sauce.

REFERENCES

Apicius: *On Cooking*.
Celsus: *On Medicine*.
Cicero: *Letters to His Friends; On Fate*.
Friedlaender, Ludwig: *Roman Life and Manners*.
Macrobius: *Saturnalia*.
Petronius: *Satyricon*.
Plautus: *Baccaria*.
Pliny the Elder: *Natural History*.
Plutarch: *Life of: Lucullus; Antony*.
Suetonius: *Life of Augustus*.
Varro: *Antiquities of Man* (quoted by Macrobius).

4

Housing

THE ANCIENT ROMANS AT HOME

> "What is more sacred, what more inviolably hedged about by every
> kind of sanctity, than the home of every individual citizen?"
> —Cicero (*On His Own Home* 109; tr. N. H. Watts LCL)

In Roman times, as now, the size of one's living quarters depended on
the depth of one's pockets. The wealthiest Romans could afford luxurious mansions, perhaps on the Palatine Hill, one of the city's most exclu-
sive residential districts. (It is no coincidence that the English words
palace and *palatial* derive from *[mons] Palatinus*, the Latin phrase for Palatine Hill.)

The vast majority of Romans, however, lived under much more modest circumstances, often in rental property. In the squalid sections of the
city, large apartment complexes—called *insulae*—sprouted up. Although
some *insulae* were relatively comfortable, most were crowded, dirty, dangerous buildings prone to fire and collapse. Many reached six or seven
stories in height.

On the other hand, the typical private residence included some universal architectural features, such as the following:

1. The *atrium* was a rectanglar room with an open-air skylight near the front of
   the house; visitors were greeted here, and family portraits and other memen-
   tos were displayed here.

2. The *vestibulum*, "vestibule," was the entryway to the house; it led directly to the atrium.

3. The atrium generally opened out onto the *peristyle*, an open-air courtyard that functioned as the family's backyard. In the courtyard might be gardens, fountains, small statuary, and the like.

4. Surrounding the courtyard, and opening onto it, were the family's living quarters, including the *triclinium* (dining room), *culina* (kitchen), and *cubicula* (bedrooms).

Many variations and permutations of the above were possible. Pliny the Younger's two villas, described later in this chapter, are good examples of the varied floorplans that a creative architect might devise.

Building Materials The roofs of homes and other buildings were originally covered with wooden shingles. Pliny the Elder (A.D. 23–79) asserted that oak was the best kind of wood to use for this purpose, followed by beech, and then pine. In the third century B.C., wooden shingles gradually fell out of favor and terracotta tiles became the preferred roofing material (Pliny the Elder *Natural History* 16.36).

ISSUES OF CITY LIFE

Lack of Urban Planning After the sack of Rome by the Gauls in 387 B.C. the city was rebuilt quickly, without much regard to planning, especially in residential areas. Livy (59 B.C.–A.D. 17) asserts that the government supplied materials such as roof tiles to any citizens who requested them; it also allowed citizens to quarry stone and cut timber without limitation. No attention was devoted to constructing straight streets; individuals built homes on vacant lots without first ascertaining if someone else owned the property. The sewers of Rome, which originally were designed to run under public streets, later flowed directly under private homes, because these dwellings were constructed so hastily that the builders either did not check for subterranean sewer lines or did not care (Livy *From the Founding of the City* 5.55).

Fire and Water Fires were a constant threat to the poorly constructed *insulae* of Rome's inner city, as Juvenal (ca. A.D. 60–ca. A.D. 130) indicates:

But here we inhabit a city supported for the most part by slender props; for that is how the [landlord] holds up the tottering house, patches up gaping cracks in the old wall, bidding the inmates sleep at ease under a roof ready to tumble about their ears. No, no, I must live where there are no fires, no nightly alarms. [A fire starts on the ground floor.] Ucalegon [a third floor resident] below is already shouting for water and [moving his worthless possessions, in an effort to save them from the flames]; smoke is pouring out of your third floor attic, but you know nothing of it, for if the alarm begins in the ground floor, the last man to burn will be he who has nothing to shelter him from the rain but the [roof] tiles. (Juvenal *Satires* 3.193–202; tr. G. G. Ramsay LCL)

Juvenal also refers to the *altae fenestrae* ("windows high up," [6.31]) and the *tecta sublima* ("lofty roofs," 3.269) of the typically towering apartment building. Martial (*Epigrams* 1.117) mentions that he resides on the third floor of his apartment building and that the climb is a steep one, if *scala alta* ("high steps") is an accurate indication.

Fire was not the only phenomenon that threatened the occupants of the *insulae*. Tacitus describes the calamitous flooding of the Tiber River in A.D. 69; the waters were so high above flood stage that they penetrated into areas of the city that were generally immune to watery encroachments. The result: apartment buildings—Tacitus does not specify the number, but significant destruction is implied—collapsed because of foundations weakened by the standing water (Tacitus *Histories* 1.86).

Fire Sale. A first century B.C. man of wealth, Marcus Licinius Crassus, had a unique method of increasing his net worth. Crassus knew of the susceptibility of *insulae* to fire and collapse, so he devised a plan to benefit from the situation.

First, he acquired an army of over 500 slaves trained in architecture and construction. Then, whenever he learned of a fire ravaging the inner city, he would appear at the site with his slaves. The frantic owner of the property could generally be counted on to sell at a ridiculously low price, as (in an era before the dawn of the insurance industry) he would stand to lose a considerable amount of money should his property be reduced to ashes.

So Crassus would purchase the burning buildings on the spot, instruct his slaves (also versed in fire control) to extinguish the blaze, and salvage whatever he could. "In this way," says Plutarch, "the largest part of Rome came into his possession" (Plutarch *Life of Crassus* 2).

Cicero (106–43 B.C.) also owned property in the city, but he (like many such owners) constantly found himself dealing with the consequences of faulty construction. In a letter to Atticus he complains that "two of [his] shops have fallen down and the rest are cracking: so not only the tenants, but even the mice, have migrated" (Cicero *Letters to Atticus* 14.9). He goes on to say that not all is lost, for he has a plan for rebuilding that will transform his setbacks into future gain.

Rents in Rome may have been quadruple the rates found in other parts of Italy. The historian Dio Cassius describes an incident of civil strife in Italy (41 B.C.), one of the byproducts of which was the destruction of many homes and apartments in Rome and elsewhere. As a result, Roman renters who lost their domiciles received a government rebate of 2,000 sesterces (presumably the sum paid for one year's rent), whereas outlanders were given one-fourth that amount.

The cost of renting seems to have been comparably higher over a century earlier. When Ptolemy VI, deposed king of Egypt, made his way to Rome in 163 B.C., he stayed in Rome with an artist named Demetrius, a man he had met in Alexandria. But Demetrius, despite his relatively remunerative profession, was consigned to a tiny, sparsely furnished rooming house; it was all that he could afford in an era of high rents (Dio Cassius *Roman History* 48.9; Diodorus Siculus *Library of History* 31. 18).

Unruly Livestock   In 191 B.C., a couple of domesticated cattle somehow wandered into a house, meandered up the stairs, and appeared on the roof of the building. It was a bad bovine move, given that the soothsayers ordered that the stairclimber animals be burned and their ashes scattered into the Tiber River (Livy *From the Founding of the City* 36.37).

Noise   The philosopher Seneca (4 B.C.–A.D. 65 had the misfortune to live directly above a public bathing establishment. Many kinds of sounds, therefore, wafted their way up to his unwilling ears. In one of his epistles he describes some of these auditory "delights" and their sources:

The weight lifters: grunting and groaning as they pump the iron, or pretend to, and once they finish a set of repetitions, the breath they have been holding they release with a loud hiss.

The massage recipients: their masseuses create slapping noises as they work on their clients' backs. The ballplayers: shouting and calling out their scores. Thieves: when caught in the act, they add to the shouting. Bathers, who like to sing at the tops of their lungs. Swimmers with an affinity for "cannonball" dives. Hairpluckers, who loudly drum up business with shrieking voices, and the customers of same, whose yelps fill the building with each depilation. Fast-food vendors, in all their stentorian splendor, who vie with one another in the endless competition for diners. (Seneca *Moral Epistles* 56)

Haunted Houses. In a letter to his friend Licinius Sura, Pliny the Younger (A.D. 62–ca. 112) describes several examples of ghostly sightings in houses. In the first instance he relates the experiences of Curtius Rufus, a military aide to a Roman governor of Africa. One day just prior to his departure for the province, he was walking along the portico of his house when he saw—much to his astonishment—the image of a woman. And not just any woman, but larger than life and exceedingly beautiful. She claimed to be "the spirit of Africa" and said that she was appearing to him to predict his future: namely, that when he returned to Rome after his service to the governor, he himself would hold a high government office, would later become the governor of Africa, and would ultimately meet his end there. Everything played out precisely as the ghost had foretold.

Pliny goes on to write that the same eerie creature appeared to Rufus when he arrived in Africa to take up his governorship. Later, when he became ill, he assumed that his ailment would be fatal (even though in reality that was not the case); but so certain was he that the ghost's prediction about his demise in Africa would come to pass that he made no effort to regain his health, and so he ultimately died in Africa (Pliny the Younger *Letters* 7.27).

COUNTRY RESIDENCES

In 54 B.C., Cicero wrote a progress report to his brother Quintus (then in Gaul) about his country house, under construction at the time. **A House under Construction**

When Cicero arrived at the construction site, he noted with some disgust that the architect, a man named Diphilus, was not showing much industriousness, even though the house was virtually complete; only the baths, a walkway, and an aviary needed to be built. The colonnade looked impressive, requiring only a few finishing touches, and the paving of the walks was also nearing completion. Cicero did note a couple of arched roofs that were unsatisfactory, and he ordered Diphilus to make them right. He himself made an alteration in the bathroom, moving the stove from one corner to the other because, as he says, "it was so placed that its steam-pipe, from which flames break out, was exactly under the bedrooms."

On the other hand, he thought that an antechamber and the bedrooms were well designed, practical, and attractive. However, he also discovered that some of the columns that Diphilus had used in the interior were not perpendicular, nor were they properly aligned; remedial work would definitely be required! Cicero's sarcastic comment: "Some day or other he will learn the use of the plumbline and the tape." Cicero clearly did not trust Diphilus to work unsupervised, for he assured his brother that their mutual acquaintance, Caesius, would remain at the job site to make sure that the work would be done, and done correctly—he hoped within a few months.

In the same letter Cicero describes for his brother a visit he paid to Quintus's country villa, located somewhere near Arpinum (the exact site is unknown). Ironically, Quintus had never seen this villa, for it had been recently purchased for him by Cicero, from a certain Fufidius, for the tidy sum of 100,000 sesterces. It was chiefly desirable because of the many shade trees surrounding it and its numerous freshwater springs. Cicero suggested that it would be the perfect weekend getaway, with the addition of a fish pond, an exercise area, and a few grapevines (Cicero *Letters to His Brother Quintus* 3.1).

Nero's "Golden House"   "Ah! At last I can begin to live like a human being!" So said the emperor Nero (ruled A.D. 54–68) upon moving into his Domus Aurea ("Golden House"), succinctly described by Suetonius:

Its size and splendor will be sufficiently indicated by the following details. Its vestibule was large enough to contain a colossal statue of the emperor a hundred and twenty feet high; and it was so extensive that it had a triple colonnade a mile long. There was a pond, too, like a sea, surrounded with buildings to represent cities, besides tracts of country, varied by tilled fields, vineyards, pastures and woods, with great numbers of wild and domestic animals. In the rest of the house, all parts were overlaid with gold and adorned with gems and mother-of-pearl. There were dining-rooms with fretted ceilings of ivory, whose panels could turn and shower down flowers and were fitted with pipes for sprinkling the guests with perfumes. The main banquet hall was circular and constantly revolved day and night, like the heavens. He had baths supplied with sea water and sulphur water. (Suetonius *Life of Nero* 31; tr. J. C. Rolfe LCL)

An Agricultural Investment   Pliny the Younger (A.D. 62–ca. 112) wrote a letter to his friend and fellow townsman Calvisius Rufus, with a request for the latter's advice on his proposed purchase of a home and some land adjoining his estate in Comum. He saw several advantages to concluding the transaction, especially the practicality of having both estates managed and tended by the same staff of overseers, gardeners, and other laborers. He was also attracted by the fertility and productivity of the soil, which would yield a good return—particularly the vineyards.

On the other hand, Pliny thought that perhaps the vagaries of wind and weather might make for some bad harvests (thus saddling him with a monetary loss), and he also knew that the previous owner had been a poor manager, both agriculturally and fiscally.

The purchase price? A mere 3,000,000 sesterces—not bad, considering that the original asking price was 5,000,000. And Pliny asserted that he could easily lay his hands on the 3,000,000, by liquidating some of his investments and by tapping his wealthy mother-in-law for a loan for the rest (Pliny the Younger *Letters* 3.19).

A Country Estate   Pliny the Younger owned several homes in fashionable districts near Rome. The one described in the following letter was located near Laurentum, about 15 miles from Rome:

The house is large enough for my needs, but not expensive to keep up. It opens into a hall, unpretentious but not without dignity, and then there are two colonnades, rounded like the letter D, which enclose a small but pleasant courtyard. This makes a splendid retreat in bad weather, being protected by windows and still more by the overhanging roof. Opposite the middle of it is a cheerful inner hall, and then a dining-room which really is rather fine: it runs out toward the shore, and whenever the sea is driven inland by the south-west wind it is lightly washed by the spray of the spent breakers. It has folding doors or windows as large as the doors all round, so that at the front and sides it seems to look out on to three seas, and at the back has a view through the inner hall, the courtyard with the two colonnades, then the entrance-hall to the woods and mountains in the distance.

To the left of this and a little farther back from the sea is a large bedroom, and another smaller one which lets in the morning sunshine with one window and holds the last rays of the evening sun with the other; from this window too is a view of the sea beneath, this time at a safe distance. In the angle of this room and the dining-room is a corner which retains and intensifies the concentrated warmth of the sun, and this is the winter-quarters and gymnasium of my household, for no winds can be heard there except those which bring the rain clouds, and the place can still be used after the weather has broken. Round the corner is a room built round in an apse to let in the sun as it moves round and shines in each window in turn, and with one wall fitted with shelves like a library to hold the books which I read and read again. Next comes a bedroom-wing on the other side of a passage which has a floor raised and fitted with pipes to receive hot steam and circulate it at a regulated temperature. The remaining rooms on this side of the house are kept for the use of my slaves and freedmen, but most of them are quite presentable enough to receive guests.

On the other side of the dining-room is an elegantly decorated bedroom and then one which can either be a large bedroom or a moderate-sized dining room and enjoys the bright light of the sun reflected from the sea; behind is another room with an antechamber, high enough to be cool in summer and protected as a refuge in winter, for it is sheltered from every wind. A similar room and antechamber are divided off by a single wall. Then comes the cooling-room of the bath, which is large and spacious and has two curved baths built out of opposite walls; these are quite large enough if you consider that the sea is so near. Next come the oiling-room, the furnace-room, and the hot-room for the bath, and then two rest-rooms, beautifully decorated in a simple style, leading to the heated swimming-bath which is much admired and from which swimmers can see the sea. Close by is the ball-court which receives the full warmth of the setting sun. Here there is a second storey, with two living-rooms below and two above, as well as a dining-room which commands the whole expanse of sea and stretch of shore with all its lovely houses. Elsewhere another upper storey contains a room which receives both the rising and setting sun, and a good-sized wine-store and granary behind, while below is a dining-room where nothing is known of a high sea but the sound of the breakers, and even that as a dying murmur; it looks on to the garden and the encircling drive.

All round the drive runs a hedge of box, or rosemary to fill any gaps, for box will flourish extensively where it is sheltered by the buildings, but dries up if exposed in the open to the wind and salt spray even at a distance. Inside the inner ring of the drive is a young and shady vine pergola, where the soil is soft and yielding even to the bare foot. The garden itself is thickly planted with mulberries and figs, trees which the soil bears very well though it is less kind to others. On this side the dining-room away from the sea has a view as lovely as that of the sea itself, while from the windows of the two rooms behind it, can be seen the entrance to the house and another well-stocked kitchen garden.

Here begins a covered arcade nearly as large as a public building. It has windows on both sides, but more facing the sea, as there is one in each alternate bay on the garden side. These all stand open on a fine and windless day, and in stormy weather can safely be opened on one side or the other away from the wind. In front is a terrace scented with violets. As the sun beats down, the arcade increases its heat by reflection and not only retains the sun but keeps off the north-east wind so that it is as hot in front as it is cool behind. In the same way it checks the south-west wind, thus breaking the force of winds from wholly opposite quarters by one or the other of its sides; it is pleasant in winter but still more so in summer when the terrace is kept cool in the morning and the drive and nearer part of the garden in the afternoon, as its shadow falls shorter or longer on one side or the other while the day advances or declines. Inside the arcade, of course, there is least sunshine when the sun is blazing down on its roof, and as its open windows allow the western breezes to enter and circulate, the atmosphere is never heavy with stale air.

At the far end of the terrace, the arcade, and the garden is a suite of rooms which are really and truly my favourites, for I had them built myself. Here is a sun-parlour facing the terrace on one side, the sea on the other, and the sun on both. There is also a bedroom which has folding doors opening on to the arcade and a window looking out on the sea. Opposite the intervening wall is a beautifully designed alcove which can be thrown into the room by folding back its glass doors and curtains, or cut off from it if they are closed: it is large enough to hold a couch and two arm-chairs, and it has the sea at its foot; the neighbouring villas behind, and the woods beyond, views which can be seen separately from its many windows or blended into one. Next to it is a bedroom for use at night which neither the voices of my young slaves, the sea's murmur, nor the noise of a storm can penetrate, any more than the lightning's flash and light of day unless the shutters are open. This profound peace and seclusion are due to the dividing passage which runs between the room and the garden so that any noise is lost in the intervening space. A tiny furnace-room is built on here, and by a narrow outlet retains or circulates the heat underneath as required. Then there is an ante-room and a second bedroom, built out to face the sun and catch its rays the moment it rises, and retain them until after midday, though by then at an angle. When I retire to this suite I feel as if I have left my house altogether and much enjoy the sensation: especially during the Saturnalia [the week starting 17 December] when the rest of the roof resounds with festive cries in the holiday freedom, for I am not disturbing my household's merrymaking nor they my work.

Only one thing is needed to complete the amenities and beauty of the house— running water; but there are wells, or rather springs, for they are very near the surface. It is in fact a remarkable characteristic of this shore that wherever you dig you come upon water at once which is pure and not in the least brackish, although the sea is so near. The woods close by provide plenty of firewood, and the town of Ostia supplies us with everything else. There is also a village, just beyond the next house, which can satisfy anyone's modest needs, and here there are three baths for hire, a great convenience if a sudden arrival or too short a stay makes us reluctant to heat up the bath at home. The sea-front gains much from the pleasing variety of the houses built either in groups or far apart; from the sea or shore these look like a number of cities. The sand on the shore is sometimes too soft for walking after a long spell of fine weather, but more often it is hardened by the constant washing of the waves. The sea has admittedly few fish of any value, but it gives us excellent soles and prawns, and all inland produce is provided by the house, especially milk: for the herds collect there from the pastures whenever they seek water and shade.

And now do you think I have a good case for making this retreat my haunt and home where I love to be? You are too polite a townsman if you don't covet it! But I hope you will, for then the many attractions of my treasured house will have another strong recommendation in your company. (Pliny the Younger *Letters* 2.17, tr. Betty Radice LCL)

Pliny also owned a Tuscan villa, whose amenities he
described in a letter to his friend Domitius Apollinaris: **A Tuscan Villa**

My house is on the lower slopes of a hill but commands as good a view as if it were higher up, for the ground rises so gradually that the slope is imperceptible, and you find yourself at the top without noticing the climb. . . .

In front of the colonnade is a terrace laid out with box hedges clipped into different shapes, from which a bank slopes down, also with figures of animals cut out of box facing each other on either side. On the level below there is a bed of acanthus so soft one could say it looks like water. . . .

From the end of the colonnade projects a dining-room: through its folding doors it looks on to the end of the terrace, the adjacent meadow, and the stretch of open country beyond, while from its windows on one side can be seen part of the terrace and the projecting wing of the house, on the other the tree-tops in the enclosure of the adjoining riding-ground. . . . In the center a fountain plays in a marble basin, watering the plane trees round it and the ground beneath them with its light spray. In this suite is a bedroom which no daylight, voice, nor sound can penetrate, and next to it an informal dining room where I entertain my personal friends; it looks on to the small courtyard, a wing of the colonnade, and the view from the colonnade. . . .

At the corner of the colonnade is a large bedroom facing the dining-room; some windows look out on to the terrace, others on to the meadow, while just below the windows in front is an ornamental pool, a pleasure both to see and to hear, with its water falling from a height and foaming white when it strikes the marble. . . . Then you pass through a large and cheerful dressing-room, belonging to the bath, to the cooling-room, which contains a good-sized shady swimming bath. If you want more space to swim or warmer water, there is a pool in the courtyard and a well near it to tone you up with cold water when you have had enough of the warm.

Next to the cooling-room is a temperate one which enjoys the sun's kindly warmth, though not as much as the hot room which is built out in a bay. This contains three plunging-baths, two full in the sun and one in the shade, though still in the light. Over the dressing-room is built the ball court, and this is large enough for several sets of players to take different kinds of exercise.

Not far from the bath is a staircase leading to three suites of rooms and then to a covered arcade. . . . The head of the arcade is divided off as a bedroom, from which can be seen the riding ground, the vineyard, and the mountains. Next to it is another room which has plenty of sun, especially in winter, and then comes a suite which connects the riding ground with the house. (Pliny the Younger *Letters* 5.6; tr. Betty Radice LCL)

Pliny then explains that the foregoing is a description of only the front part of the house! Farther back, a visitor would find more dining rooms and bedrooms; a partially underground arcade; the riding ground, which was surrounded by all sorts of decorative and exotic trees and shrubs; fountains; and various other amenities. One of the many bedrooms deserves special notice:

It is built of shining white marble, extended by folding doors which open straight out into greenery; its upper and lower windows all look out into more greenery above and below. A small alcove which is part of the room but separated from it contains a bed, and although it has windows in all its walls, the light inside is dimmed by the dense shade of a flourishing vine which climbs over the whole building up to the roof. There you can lie and imagine you are in a wood, but without the risk of rain. (Pliny the Younger *Letters* 5.6; tr. Betty Radice LCL)

NOTEWORTHY PRIVATE RESIDENCES IN ROME

1. *The house of Gaius Aquilius Gallus.* Gallus, praetor in 66 B.C., owned a home on the Viminal Hill that was considered "by far the finest house of that period," surpassing the celebrated Palatine mansions belonging to Marcus Licinius Crassus and Quintus Lutatius Catulus. Although Gallus was a respected jurist and lawyer, he was even more famous for the home that he owned (Pliny the Elder *Natural History* 17.2).

2. *Cicero's house.* Cicero's Palatine home commanded an excellent view of nearly the entire city. But such a beautiful residence in one of Rome's priciest neighborhoods did not come cheaply; when Cicero closed the deal in 62 B.C., it set him back 3,500,000 sesterces. He had to borrow 2,000,000 toward the purchase price from Publius Cornelius Sulla (which caused tongues to wag, as Sulla was at the time under investigation for complicity in the Catilinarian conspiracy, an armed revolution masterminded by the dissolute politician Catiline [d. 62 B.C.]. The transaction dented Cicero's wallet to such a degree that he lamented (in a letter to Publius Sestius in December 62): "I am so heavily in debt that I am eager to join a conspiracy, if anybody would let me in."

A few years later, when Cicero was exiled from Rome, as a result of the political machinations of his rival, Publius Clodius, his 3.5 million sesterce home was leveled by Clodius's thugs (Cicero *On His Own Home* 100; *Letters to His Friends* 5.6; Aulus Gellius *Attic Nights* 12.12).

3. *The house of Lucius Licinius Crassus.* Crassus, consul in 95 B.C. and censor in 92, owned a Palatine home valued at 1,000,000 sesterces. It boasted—among other amenities—six imported marble columns in the atrium, and grounds beautified by numerous, carefully cultivated trees. Pliny the Elder states that some of these trees had survived until being burned in the great fire of A.D. 64, thus giving them a lifespan of at least 160 years.

Pliny also relates that in his censorial year Crassus was constantly criticized by his colleague, Gnaeus Domitius Ahenobarbus, for his luxurious lifestyle, unbecoming for a censor. The envious Domitius offered to relieve Crassus of this charge by buying Crassus's home for 1,000,000 sesterces. Crassus agreed to the offer, under the condition that he be allowed to retain ownership of six of the trees. Domitius retorted that he would not pay one thin *denarius* for the property unless all the trees were included.

Crassus's reply: "Well, then, Domitius, am I the one who is setting the bad example, . . . I, who live quite unpretentiously in the house that came to me by inheritance, or is it you, who price six trees at a million sesterces?" (Pliny the Elder *Natural History* 17.3–4).

4. *The house of Hortensius.* The noted first century B.C. orator/gourmand Quintus Hortensius Hortalus owned a home on the Palatine that was (uncharacteristically?) unassuming. It was neither large nor elegantly furnished, featuring short, inexpensive columns; it completely lacked decorative marbles or costly, mosaic floors. The house was later occupied by the emperor Augustus (Suetonius *Life of Augustus* 72).

5. *The house of Drusus.* Marcus Livius Drusus, tribune in 91 B.C., hired an architect to design and build a home for him on the Palatine Hill. The (unnamed) architect offered to devise a floor plan that would afford maximum security and privacy. Drusus replied that on the contrary, his house must be built in such a way that everything he did would be open to public scrutiny.

Cicero's house (#2 above) was later constructed on the site occupied by the house of Drusus (Velleius Paterculus *Compendium of Roman History* 2.14).

6. *The house of Capitolinus.* Marcus Manlius Capitolinus, lionized in 387 B.C. for saving Rome from a Gallic invasion but demonized three years later for allegedly attempting to establish a monarchy, owned a home on the Capitoline Hill. After his condemnation in 384, his house was razed; it was further decreed that in the future, no patrician should dwell on the Capitoline Hill (Livy *From the Founding of the City* 6.20).

7. *Pliny's house.* Pliny the Younger (A.D. 62–ca. 112) owned a home on the Esquiline Hill, formerly the residence of the first century A.D. Albinovanus Pedo. Martial mentions having written a little book of poetry for Pliny and having it delivered from the seedier section of town where he (Martial) lived, up the "steep path" to the heights of the Esquiline, a much more fashionable district (Martial *Epigrams* 10.19).

8. *Pompey's houses.* Pompey (106–48 B.C.) originally owned a house on the Carinae, between the Caelian and Esquiline Hills. This house became noted for its unique interior decorations: prows of foreign ships captured by Pompey during his various military campaigns. Later, he built a new residence for himself near the theater that bears his name. But even this house was unpretentious, at least for a man sporting the cognomen Magnus ("Great"). In fact, it was so ordinary that the subsequent owner, upon first inspecting it, was astonished at its relatively small size and wondered aloud where Pompey ate his meals (Cicero *Philippics* 2.68; Velleius Paterculus *Compendium of Roman History* 2.77; Plutarch *Life of Pompey* 40).

THE LAST WORD ON HOMES

Cicero had some choice comments on the selection of a home:

I must discuss what sort of house a man of rank and station should have. Its prime object is serviceableness. To this the plan of the building should be adapted; and yet careful attention should be paid to its convenience and distinction.

We have heard that Gnaeus Octavius—the first of that family to be elected consul—distinguished himself by building upon the Palatine an attractive and imposing house. Everybody went to see it, and it was thought to have gained votes for the owner, a new man, in his canvass for the consulship. That house Scarus demolished, and on its site he built an addition to his own house. Scaurus . . . brought to the same house, when enlarged, not only defeat, but disgrace and ruin. The truth is, a man's dignity may be enhanced by the house he lives in, but not wholly secured by it; the owner should bring honor to his house, not the house to its owner. And, as in everything else, a man must have regard not for himself alone but for others also, so in the home of a distinguished man, in which numerous guests must be entertained and crowds of every sort of people received, care must be taken to have it spacious. But if it is not frequented by visitors, if it has an air of lonesomeness, a spacious palace often becomes a discredit to its owner. (Cicero *On Duties* 1.138–139; tr. Walter Miller LCL).

REFERENCES

Aulus Gellius: *Attic Nights.*
Cicero: *Letters to Atticus; Letters to His Brother Quintus; Letters to His Friends; On Duties; On His Own Home; Philippics.*

Dio Cassius: *Roman History*.
Diodorus Siculus: *Library of History*.
Juvenal: *Satires*.
Livy: *From the Founding of the City*.
Martial: *Epigrams*.
Pliny the Elder: *Natural History*.
Pliny the Younger: *Letters*.
Plutarch: *Life of Crassus; Life of Pompey*.
Seneca: *Moral Epistles*.
Suetonius: *Life of Augustus; Life of Nero*.
Tacitus: *Histories*.
Velleius Paterculus: *Compendium of Roman History*.

5

Travel

THE ROMANS ON THE ROAD

Getting from here to there was a concern of many Romans: soldiers on the march from one end of the far-flung Roman dominions to the other; wealthy citizens indulging in weekend getaways to their rural villas, or perhaps to fashionable vacation retreats such as Baiae or Praeneste; tourists traveling to Greece or Egypt to see the monuments and artwork, or to attend lectures by noted scholars; couriers and messengers hurrying with letters or communiqués from important government officials to their counterparts stationed hundreds of miles from Rome. Sometimes certain Romans embarked unwillingly on journeys, as a result of banishment decrees because of some crime they may have committed.

To respond to the needs of an increasingly mobile Roman populace, a sophisticated network of paved roads was created; traces of these roads still exist in virtually all the areas of western Europe once occupied or controlled by the Romans. Although the road system was built primarily for the use of the army, civilians also frequented it.

Travelers might walk, or ride in wagons, or ride on horses, mules, or donkeys; the rich and ostentatious were carried in litters.

Overland travel, however, was slow and often dangerous. Thieves and muggers, seemingly lurking behind every tree and boulder, awaited the weak and unwary. So river and ocean transit was the preferred method of getting from one place to another. Some travelers might use a combination of both modes; for example, those traveling from Rome to

Greece or points east could make their way down to Brundisium (in southern Italy) via the Appian Way and then book passage on a sea-going vessel for the remainder of the trip.

Bringing Produce to Market

Farmers would sometimes bring their produce into the city to sell it; the conveyance might be a heavy, four-wheeled wagon called a *raeda*. Martial (ca. A.D. 40–ca. 104) describes the food typically found in one: leafy, green cabbages; leeks; lettuce; beets; thrushes; a hare; and a pig. To prevent breakage while in transit, eggs were carried by a runner (*cursor*) who walked or jogged in front of the wagon, the eggs safely nestled in a bundle of straw that he carried.

Heavy wagons like *raedae* generally had to be unloaded at the city gates, for their use on Rome's streets was prohibited, at least during daylight hours. Juvenal (ca. A.D. 60–ca. 130) complained that sleep was impossible because of the noise in the streets caused in part by the nocturnal wheeled traffic (Martial *Epigrams* 3.47; Juvenal *Satires* 3.236–238; Scriptores Historiae Augustae *Life of Hadrian* 21). Martial mentions the *raeda* in connection with a certain Bassus, who took his groceries from Rome to his country estate because the estate's produce gardens were barren.

Delivering the Mail

Prolific epistlers such as Cicero (106–43 B.C.) employed professional letter carriers (*tabellarii*) to transport messages to their correspondents. (There was no universal postal service in the modern sense of the term.) These *tabellarii* prided themselves on their efficiently prompt service, sometimes to the point of obnoxiousness. Cicero complains about this in a letter to Cassius; the letter carriers are in such a hurry to get on the road that they leave Cicero no time to compose a decent letter. They appear at his doorstep *petasati*, "ready to roll" (literally, wearing *petasati*, broad-brimmed hats used to shelter a traveler's face and neck from the blazing sun). So Cicero apologizes to Cassius for the brevity of this particular letter; he was rushed by the *tabellarii* (Cicero *Letters to His Friends* 15.17). Suetonius (ca. A.D. 69–140) mentions that the emperor Augustus was partial to wearing a *petasatus* whenever he ventured outside on a sunny day and that when he traveled any distance he was carried in a litter—but at a very slow pace; two days, for example, were required to cover the 23 miles from Rome to Praeneste. Augustus's preferred method of transport: by sea (Suetonius *Life of Augustus* 82).

Measuring Mileage

Vitruvius (first century A.D.) provides a detailed description of the ancient Roman version of an odometer:

By this contrivance . . . we can learn how many miles we have covered. It is as follows. The wheels of the carriage [*raeda*] are to be 4 feet in diameter, and on one wheel a point is to be marked. When the wheel begins to move forward from this point and to revolve on the road surface, it will have completed a distance of 12½ feet. . . .

The next step: let a drum be secured to the inner side of the hub of the wheel with one tooth projecting. . . . Above this, in the body of the carriage, let a box be securely fixed with a drum revolving perpendicularly, and fastened to an axle. On the outside edge of the drum 400 teeth are to be set at equal intervals so as to meet the teeth on the lower drum. Further, at the side of the upper drum there is to be fixed a second tooth projecting beyond the other teeth.

Now above there is to be placed a horizontal wheel toothed in the same manner, and enclosed in a similar case, with teeth which fit upon the single tooth which projects on the side of the second drum. In this drum openings are to be made in number equal to the miles which can be covered with the carriage in a day. . . . In all these openings, round stones are to be placed [in such a way that they] can fall one by one into the carriage body and a bronze vessel which is placed below.

Thus, when the wheel moves forwards, and carries with it the lowest drum, in a single revolution, the wheel causes its one tooth to strike in passing the teeth in the upper drum. The effect will be that when the lower drum has revolved 400 times, the upper drum will revolve once . . . as [the upper drum revolves once], it will record thereby a distance of 5000 feet [i.e., a Roman mile]. Hence, when a stone falls, it will announce by its sound the traversing of a single mile, and the number of the stones collected from below will indicate, by their total, the number of miles for the day's journey. (Vitruvius *On Architecture* 10.9; tr. Frank Granger LCL)

Traveling Man. According to Pliny the Elder, the emperor Tiberius (ruled A.D. 14–37) held the record for swiftness of overland travel. He once covered 182 miles in 24 hours on a hasty journey to Germany to visit his ill brother, Drusus (Pliny the Elder *Natural History* 7.84).

Mark Antony (82–30 B.C.) spared no expense on those occasions when he hit the road. According to **Traveling in Style** Plutarch, his travel arrangements rivaled those that might be made for a triumphant general: numerous attendants preceding and following; elaborate tents for overnight accommodations; expensive picnic dinners, often consumed in picturesque settings, such as in woodlands or on riverbanks; wagons and chariots pulled by lions; and perhaps worst of all, the commandeering of private homes for the use of musicians and ladies of the evening (Plutarch *Life of Mark Antony* 9).

The emperor Commodus (ruled A.D. 180–192) traveled in style. The carriages in which he rode had intricately carved wheel decorations and seats that swiveled, enabling the riders to face or avoid the sun or the wind as they pleased. He also had carriages equipped with odometers and sundials, and "still others designed for the indulgence of his vices" (Scriptores Historiae Augustae *Life of Pertinax* 8).

**A Roman
Superhighway**

The Appian Way (despite Horace's complaints about its discomforts) was undoubtedly the most celebrated and most admired paved road in the ancient Roman network of highways. Five centuries after Horace (65–8 B.C.) lamented its few amenities and many irritants such as the oppressively hot sun, infrequent rest stops, fearless muggers, and virtually no relief from the incessant humming of aggressive, lightning-quick mosquitos, the Appian Way still cheerfully bore travelers and their conveyances (Horace *Satires* 1.5). The sixth century A.D. author Procopius noted that a determined traveler could traverse the distance from Rome to Capua in five days on the Appian Way, and that the road was sufficiently wide to permit two wagons traveling in opposite directions to pass each other without necessitating any tricky maneuvers by their drivers. The heavy polygonal stones with which the road was paved were cut and polished with such precision that they could be permanently set in place without cement or mortar. And they fit together so snugly that they appeared to be one vast, uninterrupted sheet of stone, not individual blocks. Even after some 800 years of existence, the road still looked as fresh and finished as the day its construction was completed in the fourth century B.C. (Procopius *History of the Wars* 5.14).

In the second century B.C. the tribune Gaius Sempronius Gracchus initiated some road construction projects, incorporating the same exacting standards as those applied to the Appian Way. Gracchus (like most Roman road builders) believed that the shortest distance between two points was a straight line, and he planned his roads accordingly. Valleys were bridged, low spots were filled, and both sides of his roads were constructed to the same height, so that they took on a pleasingly symmetrical appearance. He also placed stone mile markers at the appropriate places and set "other stones, too . . . on both sides of the road, in order that equestrians might be able to mount their horses from them and have no need of assistance" (Plutarch *Life of Gaius Gracchus* 7; tr. Bernadotte Perrin LCL).

A TRIP FROM LUGDUNUM TO ROME

The fifth century A.D. Christian poet Sidonius Apollinaris described a journey he undertook to Rome from Lugdunum (in France, modern Lyons). The first part of the venture seemed to proceed well, and in fact Sidonius's only "complaint" pertained to the many friends he met along the way, who delayed him through their hospitality. He very briefly recounted the crossing of the Alps Mountains and the descent into Italy, a section of the trip made partially on horseback and partially by boat. Sidonius seemed to particularly enjoy river travel, if his keen observations were indicative of his attitude: "[The banks of the rivers of Italy] were everywhere clad with groves of oak and maple. A concert of birds filled the air with sweet sounds; their nest structures quivered, balanced sometimes on hollow reeds, sometimes on prickly rushes, sometimes too on smooth bulrushes; for all this undergrowth . . . had sprouted confusedly along the river banks."

He next made his way to Ravenna, and from there to the Po River, which was so briny and polluted that drinking from it was out of the question. Next stop: the Rubicon River, famous as the boundary between Gaul and Italy. (By crossing it in 49 B.C. with his army intact, Julius Caesar precipitated a civil war; his words "the die is cast" have attained immortality.)

Eventually Sidonius entered onto the Via Flaminia (Flaminian Way, one of the chief north-south routes in Italy), where disaster struck in the form of a flu-like illness; he described the malady as causing alternating fits of sweating and chills. "Meanwhile, fever and thirst made havoc of the innermost recesses of my heart and marrow; to their greedy claims, I kept promising . . . the deliciousness of springs . . . wells, and streams . . . but caution ever balked my longing."

Finally, Rome! "I thought I could drink dry not only its aqueducts but the ponds used in its mock sea-fights." But his faith in God enabled him to recover from his illness without draining the aqueducts, and he eventually found a place to stay, where he had the leisure time to compose the description of his journey (Sidonius Apollinaris *To Heronius* 1.5; tr. W. B. Anderson LCL).

A TRIP FROM THE ADRIATIC TO ROME

Tacitus recounts the journey of Gnaeus Calpurnius Piso (consul in 7 B.C.) from the northern Adriatic Sea to Rome; this trek represents a good example of the land-water combination of travel:

Piso left his vessels at Ancona and, travelling through Picenum [in northeastern Italy], then by the Flaminian Road, came up with a legion marching from Pannonia to Rome. . . . From Narnia . . . he sailed down the Nar [River], then down the Tiber, and added to the exasperation of the populace by bringing his vessel to shore at the mausoleum of the Caesars. It was a busy part of the day and of the riverside; yet, he with a marching column of retainers, and Plancina [his wife] with her escort of women, proceeded beaming on their way. (Tacitus *Annals* 3.9; tr. John Jackson LCL)

SENECA ON TRAVEL

Seneca (4 B.C.–A.D. 65) had a less than positive attitude about the supposed benefits of travel. Travel cannot:

1. restrain unhealthy desires
2. cure hotheadedness
3. cleanse the soul of evil
4. cultivate good judgment
5. help correct errors or mistakes

According to Seneca, traveling may entertain the traveler temporarily, like something strange momentarily holds the attention of a child, but long-range benefits are lacking. Not only that, but travel can be downright irritating: various physical ailments, like motion sickness, often afflict travelers, making them want to leave their destinations almost as soon as they arrive, "like birds that flit and are off as soon as they have alighted."

Travel can enlighten and inform, especially of odd or unfamiliar locales and geographical phenomena, but this sort of information does not make a person better or healthier.

Seneca's conclusion: "We ought rather to spend our time in study, and to cultivate those who are masters of wisdom, learning something which has been investigated, but not settled" (Seneca *Moral Epistles* 104; tr. Richard Gummere LCL).

Despite Seneca's distaste for traveling (apparent in the previous selection), he occasionally found himself by necessity on the road. But he traveled light; he claimed that he began a journey as if he were shipwrecked, that is, with no more possessions than a shipwrecked passenger would be expected to have.

On a two-day trip with his friend Maximus—in a farmer's wagon—he related that he took with him very few slaves and only the clothes on his back. He also packed a mattress and two rugs: one for a blanket, the other to lay on top of the mattress. (Travelers often spent their nights at inns or at homes of friends along the way, but if neither was available they would simply "camp out" by the side of the road.) Figs and bread sufficed for meals; writing tablets were deemed almost as necessary as food and so found their way into the luggage. The wagon was pulled by a pair of mules that moved so slowly that the casual observer might almost think they were dead.

Although Seneca was perfectly content with his style of traveling and, in particular, his thriftiness, he always felt somewhat embarrassed when he chanced to meet a more luxuriously equipped traveler, the kind "whose gold plate goes with him on his travels, [who] farms land in all the provinces, [who] unrolls a large account book, [who] is conveyed in decorated chariots and horses with gold trappings." Yet Seneca doubted that the rich traveler was much improved or happier because of these baubles. Cato the Elder, he noted, got around on the back of a donkey;

his luggage could always fit in a pair of modestly sized saddlebags.

Seneca concluded his travel musings by noting that whoever coined the Latin word for baggage, *impedimenta*, literally "hindrances," certainly knew whereof he spoke (Seneca *Moral Epistles* 87; tr. Richard Gummere LCL).

Seneca elsewhere (*Moral Epistles* 123) alluded to his late-night arrival at his Alban villa after a short but fatiguing journey. When he entered the house, he discovered to his annoyance that neither his cook nor his baker had prepared any food for him. So he overcame his exhaustion and hunger by sitting down at his desk and writing.

Later in the same epistle, he described the modern traveler as someone who considers it demeaning to embark on a journey without an army of retainers to clear the road ahead, or to leave home without mules loaded down with expensively carved and decorated drinking cups. Baggage that can be jostled and knocked about with no danger to its contents is baggage not worth taking on a trip.

Seneca's advice: "You should avoid conversation with all such persons; they are the sort that communicate and engraft their bad habits from one to another" (*Moral Epistles* 123; tr. Richard Gummere LCL).

TRAVEL BY SEA

The Roman poet Ovid (43 B.C.–A.D. 17) was banished from Rome in A.D. 9 by the emperor Augustus. The precise cause for his exile has long been a matter of great interest to scholars and historians. Ovid himself gave two reasons—*carmen et error*, "a poem and a mistake"—but no details. So we are left to guess which poem and what kind of mistake. They must have been serious, however, because Augustus sent Ovid to Tomis, an isolated outpost on the frigid northern shore of the Black Sea. There, the miserable poet lived out the final years of his life, despite numerous entreaties to Augustus to suspend or at least alleviate his punishment.

Ovid's Unhappy Voyage to Tomis

Ovid describes the sea voyage from Rome to Tomis in several poetic entries in *Tristia*, or "Sad Poems" (Ovid *Tristia* 1.1–4, 10–11):

Apparently the order for Ovid to leave Rome came swiftly, for he laments that he had no time to ready slaves or other potential companions, or even to pack any clothing. His wife would not be accompanying him into exile—their plan was for her to stay in Rome to agitate for his recall, a plan that never succeeded—while his daughter, living at the time in Libya, had not even been notified of her father's fate. So it was a tearful farewell on their doorstep, a parting ordeal that Ovid likens to the sorrow felt by the Trojans when Troy was captured and sacked.

The ship carrying Ovid to exile made its way down the western coast of Italy before turning eastward, toward the Adriatic Sea, where they encountered a violent storm. Ovid asserts that the mountain-sized waves created troughs between them so deep that the sand on the ocean floor was actually visible and sucked up by and into the hurricane-force winds. And as for the ship's captain? His terrified facial expression said it all! He had completely lost control of his craft—like a mounted rider who cannot control his horse and lets the reins dangle. So the ship was at the mercy of the elements, buffeted furiously by the winds and waves.

And then a new problem arose. The wind began blowing the ship westward toward the coast of Italy, forbidden territory for Ovid. The poet describes his conflicting emotions: happy at what might be his forced return to Italian soil, but worried about violating the emperor's command to be forever gone.

Eventually the storm subsided, the ship did not careen back toward Italy, and the remainder of the first part of the voyage—to Greece—was completed without further incident. When Ovid reached Corinth he disembarked, crossed the Isthmus, and boarded a second ship called the *Minerva*. Ovid notes that *Minerva* is an excellent vessel, one that cuts through the water smoothly whether the power source be wind in the sails or oars in the water. In fact, the ship is so swift that it not only leaves in its wake others that left port at the same time but even overtakes those that departed hours earlier. And although several storms lay in the ship's watery path to the Hellespont, *Minerva* weathered them unscathed.

Minerva passed through the Hellespont and dropped off its famous passenger in Thrace, where he determined to continue his journey on foot through the territory of the Bistones, an indigenous race of Thracian people. He wonders which is worse: to drown in a storm at sea, or to be set upon and killed by the murderous muggers who, he is certain, are to be found behind every Thracian rock and bush.

Ultimately he probably suffered the worst fate of all: to survive the rigors of the journey, and arrive safely in Tomis.

Transporting Oversize Cargo During the reign of the emperor Caligula (ruled A.D. 37–41) a gigantic obelisk was transported from Egypt to Rome. Because the Roman commercial fleet did not possess a ship large enough to convey the obelisk, a special vessel had to be built for the purpose. This ship had a fir tree mast with a diameter so large that it required four men with arms extended to encircle it; the cost of the mast alone was put at 80,000 sesterces. The ship "carried one hundred and twenty bushels of lentils for ballast, and its length took up a large part of the left side of the harbor at Ostia, for under the emperor Claudius, it was sunk there, with three moles [piers] as high as towers erected upon it" (Pliny the Elder *Natural History* 16.201–202; tr. H. Rackham LCL).

REFERENCES

Cicero: *Letters to His Friends*.
Horace: *Satires*.
Juvenal: *Satires*.
Martial: *Epigrams*.
Ovid: *Tristia*.
Pliny the Elder: *Natural History*.
Plutarch: *Life of Gaius Gracchus; Life of Mark Antony*.
Procopius: *History of the Wars*.
Scriptores Historiae Augustae: *Life of Hadrian; Life of Pertinax*.
Seneca: *Moral Epistles*.
Sidonius Apollinaris: *To Heronius*.
Suetonius: *Life of Augustus*.
Tacitus: *Annals*.
Vitruvius: *On Architecture*.

6

Politics

ROMAN GOVERNMENT AND LAW

Monarchy . . . Republic . . . Empire . . . the ancient Romans lived under all three forms of government during their civilization's long history. Kings—seven of them—ruled from ca. 753 to 509 B.C. After the abolition of the monarchy, a republican system was implemented in which the top executive officials—consuls—were elected annually and always in pairs, the idea being that each consul would serve as a check on the other's ambitions.

The Republic gave way to the Empire in the late first century B.C. While Rome remained a republic in name and even retained many of the same offices and political traditions, rule by one man (unelected) was clearly the hallmark of the Roman imperial system. Augustus is generally regarded as Rome's first emperor, although Julius Caesar or Tiberius might also qualify for that distinction.

The Roman senate (the term derives from *senes*, "old men," because its members were usually drawn from the ranks of elder statesmen) was always a respected element of the government, even though it possessed few specifically designated powers. Unlike its modern counterpart, its members were not elected by popular vote but rather were chosen by the ranking magistrates; former consuls and other high officials generally qualified for admission automatically. The Roman senate had no legislative function; rather, it was primarily an advisory body. However, because it was composed largely of distinguished, respected, powerful men, its advice on matters of statecraft was usually taken seriously by lawmaking assemblies and by individual politicians.

Chief Offices of the Roman Republic

- *consuls* (two elected annually): chief administrators of the government; commanded the Roman army during times of war. The replacement for a consul who died in office was called a *suffect*.

- *praetors* (the number varied; by the second century B.C. six were elected annually); administered the government when both consuls were absent; often served as presiding magistrates in court cases.

- *aediles* (four elected annually); responsibilities included overseeing road, bridge, and aqueduct repairs; supervising weights and measures; enforcing traffic laws.

- *quaestors* (like praetors, the number varied; by the first century B.C. twenty were elected annually); primarily treasury officials; often assigned to travel with the army in the field, to maintain records of expenditures and administer the payroll.

- *tribunes of the people* (initially five, later ten, elected annually); primarily responsible for protecting the interests of the plebeians; they had the right of *intercessio*—absolute veto power—over any legislation they deemed harmful to plebeian interests.

- *censors* (two elected every five years, to serve eighteen months). One of the best descriptions of censorial powers comes from the pen of Plutarch: "[their duties were] to watch, regulate, and punish any tendency to indulge in licentious or voluptuous habits . . . they had the authority to degrade a Roman knight or expel a senator [from the Roman senate]. . . . They also carried out and maintained a general census of property, kept a register of all the citizens . . . and exercised various other important powers" (Plutarch *Life of Cato the Elder* 16; tr. Ian Scott-Kilvert LCL).

A Sampling of Roman Laws

Individual magistrates, often tribunes, could propose legislation, whereupon the proposal would be debated and various opinions—especially those of senators—weighed. Then the measure would be referred to the Centuriate Assembly (the chief legislative body), where voting took place; if the proposal passed, it became law. The new law was often named after its originator (e.g., a law passed under the sponsorship of Julius Caesar would be called the Lex Julia). The following entries provide a sampling of specific Roman laws (*lex*; pl. *leges*).

Pop the Question. Prior to 445 B.C., intermarriage between patricians and plebeians was prohibited. However, in that year a tribune named Gaius Canuleius proposed a law that would outlaw the prohibition. His efforts were successful, and such marriages were henceforth permitted under the provisions of the Lex Canuleia.

There's Never a Fee, Whether We Win or Not. The Lex Cincia, passed in 204 B.C. probably at the behest of the tribune Marcus Cincius Alimentus, prohibited lawyers from accepting fees for legal services rendered to individual clients.

Cut Her Out of the Will! In 169 B.C. the tribune Quintus Voconius Saxa successfully pushed for the passage of his Lex Voconia, which limited the rights of women to receive inheritances (Cicero *Against Verres* 2.106–108; Broughton, *Magistrates of the Roman Republic* I: 425).

Dinner Bell Blues. Gaius Fannius Strabo's name would probably never appear in an ancient gourmand's hall of fame, even if such a thing existed. In 161 B.C., as consul, the strict Strabo sponsored a law—the Lex Fannia—that placed severe restrictions on the amount of money that could be spent on banquets. More specifically, a limit "of one hundred *asses* a day at the Roman and plebeian games, at the Saturnalia, and on certain other days; of thirty *asses* on ten additional days each month; but on all other days of only ten," according to Aulus Gellius (*Attic Nights* 2.24; tr. John C. Rolfe LCL). Pliny the Elder (*Natural History* 10.139) adds that the Lex Fannia permitted no fowl to be served at dinner parties except for one skinny hen.

The Lex Fannia applied to banquets and feasts in Rome only. But the rest of Italy soon fell under similar restraints, when in 141 B.C. the tribune Titus Didius engineered passage of the Lex Didia, a sort of pan-Italian version of the Lex Fannia.

Keep Out the Foreigners! In 126 B.C. the tribune Marcus Junius Pennus successfully entered into the law books his Lex Junia, which prohibited noncitizens from residing in Rome or Roman towns; it also expelled any who had already established residences.

Bridge under (Re)construction. On election days, voters had to cross over to the polls on walkways called bridges. As tribune in 119 B.C., Gaius Marius proposed a law that would narrow these bridges, presumably to make it more difficult for voters to be harangued or threatened as they prepared to cast their votes. One of the consuls, Lucius Aurelius Cotta, opposed the measure and demanded that Marius appear before the senate to defend it. Marius did just that, and although he was still a political neophyte, he immediately proclaimed that he would order Cotta to be incarcerated forthwith unless he modified his opinion on the matter. Cotta, in turn, appealed to his consular colleague, Lucius Caecilius Metellus. Metellus indicated that he agreed with Cotta's position, whereupon Marius threatened to have him arrested. Because neither consul could muster much support from the other politicians present at the time, they withdrew their opposition, and Marius's proposal subsequently became the Lex Maria (Plutarch *Life of Marius* 4).

"An Incredibly Disgraceful Law." Lucius Valerius Flaccus (suffect consul in 86 B.C.) was the author of a measure permitting debtors to repay creditors only one-fourth of the sum owed to them. Velleius Paterculus, who termed the Lex Valeria "an incredibly disgraceful law," wrote that the murder of Valerius a short time later was a "punishment he deserved" (Velleius Paterculus *Compendium of Roman History* 2.23).

The Best Seats in the House. The Lex Roscia, passed in 67 B.C. under the sponsorship of the tribune Lucius Roscius Otho, mandated that the first fourteen rows in theaters and amphitheaters be reserved for the equestrians (the upper middle class citizens) (Livy *From the Founding of the City* 99).

A Bad Law Brought Low by a Cruel Whipping. Gaius Publilius was a handsome young man of unquestioned integrity. Unfortunately, he had been given over by his father to a certain usurer named Lucius Papirius, as security for a loan. Papirius took advantage of the situation by abusing and beating young Publilius. During one of the whippings Publilius managed to escape from his tormenters and ran, bloodied, into the street.

A huge crowd soon gathered; when they heard the story that Publilius had to tell, they were irate. They ran en masse from there to the forum and then to the senate house, to demand some changes in the debtor laws; they supported their case by displaying the cut and bleeding back of Publilius to the senators.

And changes were made. No longer could creditors physically abuse or humiliate debtors, and no longer would it be legal to use human beings as collateral for loans (Livy 8.28). Livy indicates that these events occurred in 326 B.C.

THE ROMANS AS POLITICAL ANIMALS

Being Robbed Is Better Than Being Sold

Gaius Fabricius Luscinus and Publius Cornelius Rufinus both played central roles on the Roman political stage in the early third century B.C., but it would be difficult to imagine two men of such contrasting values. Fabricius was upright, honest, respectable; Rufinus, although highly regarded as a soldier and a military tactician, was dishonest and greedy. Nevertheless, when Rufinus ran for the consulship during the campaign season of 291 B.C., Fabricius supported his bid wholeheartedly because the other candidates were not comparably qualified. Although a military crisis loomed, many of Fabricius's friends were surprised that he would back Rufinus, a man whom they knew he despised. Fabricius's reply was *Malo civis me compilet quam hostis vendat*: "Better that a citizen robs me than an enemy sells me [into slavery]."

But later, when Fabricius was censor (in 275 B.C.), he felt no compunction in ejecting Rufinus from the senate on a charge of unsenatorlike extravagance: he owned 10 pounds of silver dinnerware. (Many ancient writers—Dionysius of Halicarnassus, Pliny the Elder,

Livy, Ovid, Seneca, and Plutarch among them—discuss or at least mention early Roman attitudes toward wealth and conspicuous consumption. But Aulus Gellius [*Attic Nights* 4.8] offers the most complete account of the strange bedfellows Fabricius and Rufinus. Cicero [in *On the Orator* 2.268] also refers to the story; in his version, Fabricius's famous line was addressed directly to Rufinus.)

Quintus Caecilius Metellus Macedonicus was the proud owner of a very impressive résumé: praetor in 148 B.C., consul in 143, Roman general in Greece, and later in Spain, quasher of a slave revolt, augur for the last twenty-five years of his life. But his career probably peaked in 131, when he held the office of censor. (A footnote: he and his colleague were both plebeians, the first time in Roman history that two plebeians occupied the censorship.)

A Controversial Speech on Marriage

Metellus did two things during his censorship that caused him more than a little grief. One of these deeds was his expulsion from the Roman senate of a tribune named Gaius Atinius Labeo Macerio. But more on this matter later.

The more immediate controversy erupted over a speech made by Metellus in which he said, "If we could get on without a wife, Romans, we would all avoid that annoyance, but since nature has ordained that we can neither live very comfortably with them, nor at all without them, we must take thought for our lasting well-being rather than for the pleasure of the moment" (Aulus Gellius *Attic Nights* 1.6; tr. John C. Rolfe LCL).

The reaction of Metellus's listeners ranged from puzzlement to outrage. Many noted the inconsistencies; after all, a censorial responsibility was the encouragement of stable marriages and families. To proclaim that a wife was at best an irritation, and marriage an inconvenience, seemed hardly in keeping with the august duties of the office that Metellus occupied. They pointed out that even though any marriage inevitably encounters some rough spots it has its pleasures as well, and these almost always outweigh the difficulties. Furthermore, they said, matrimonial pitfalls are exclusively the fault of the partners in the marriage and do not arise from the institution itself.

But Metellus did have at least one defender: Titus Castricius. Castricius opined that Metellus had merely spoken from the heart and had courageously articulated the truth as he saw it. What blame could anyone attach to that, especially as the speaker was a man of unquestioned honor and integrity? Furthermore, said Castricius. Metellus concluded that the efficacy of the Roman Republic depended on stable marriages, and many of them. Therefore, it was unfair to twist his words in such a way as to suggest that he was opposed to marriage.

Somehow the Republic managed to survive the squabble, and the Roman people continued to marry and propagate. Metellus's own survival, however, almost became problematic, as the previously expelled tribune, Gaius Atinius Labeo Macerio, decided to seek revenge.

Atinius had been so incensed over his ejection from the Roman senate that one day—at high noon, no less!—he set upon Metellus as that unfortunate man was walking through the middle of the city. The disgruntled tribune had every intention of avenging his being thrown out of the senate by returning the favor ... literally. He dragged Metellus to the very brink of the Tarpeian Rock and prepared to toss the censor over the edge. The gruesome deed was prevented only by the intercession of another tribune, who vetoed the imminent headlong demise of Metellus.

And as for Gaius Atinius Labeo Macerio? Pliny the Elder wryly notes that he was never called to account for his "criminal audacity." (Ancient sources on Quintus Caecilius Metellus Macedonicus are as follows: Aulus Gellius *Attic Nights* 1.6 [where, however, Gellius confuses him with his son, Quintus Caecilius Metellus Numidicus]; Pliny the Elder *Natural History* 7.142–146.)

A Consul Who Got Things Done Publius Popilius Laenas, consul in 132 B.C., was an activist politician, as the following inscription found on a milestone would suggest:

I made the road from Regium to Capua and on that road placed all the bridges, milestones, and sign-posts. From here there are 51 miles to Nuceria; 84 to Capua; 74 to Muranum; 123 to Consentia; 180 to Valentia; 231 to the strait [separating Italy from Sicily]. . . . Total from Capua to Regium 321. I also as praetor in Sicily sought out the runaways belonging to men from Italy and gave up 917 persons. Again, I was the first to cause cattle breeders to retire from public state-land in favour of plowmen. Here I put up a Market and public buildings. (*CIL* 1.638 tr. E. H. Warmington LCL)

A Two-Time Loser In 119 B.C. Gaius Marius decided to run for the aedileship, an office that by this time had been partitioned into two branches: the curule and plebeian versions (the former was regarded as more prestigious). On election day, the curule aediles (two) were elected first, and then the two plebeian aediles.

Marius announced his candidacy for the curule aedileship. However, as the votes were being tabulated it became clear to him that his bid was failing. So he quickly withdrew from that race and placed his name among those competing for the plebeian aedileship—and he lost there, too! Plutarch informs us that this unique "daily double" was unprecedented, that no Roman politician had ever been rebuffed twice on the same day.

Marius was down, but he did not stay down. In 115 he eked out a narrow praetorian victory; and then a few years later he established another electoral precedent, this one undoubtedly more personally fulfilling than the dubious one of 119: he was elected consul for five consecutive terms of office, in 104, 103, 102, 101, and 100 (Plutarch *Life of Marius* 5).

When the tribunes Lucius Apuleius Saturninus and Lucius Equitius took office on December 10 of 100 B.C., **A Bad First Day** Saturninus had already established a reputation as a fiery populist. The consular elections of that year worried Saturninus, because one of the candidates—Gaius Memmius—was a staunch opponent of Saturninus's personal choice, Gaius Servilius Glaucia. So Saturninus and Glaucia sent a gang of thugs to physically intimidate Memmius; they did their job too well—they beat him to death.

When this news made the rounds, popular indignation ran high against Saturninus, Glaucia, and quaestor/sympathizer Gaius Saufeius. So the three of them (along with their supporters) occupied by force several government buildings. But when their water supply was cut off and resistance seemed futile, they surrendered. They were temporarily confined to the senate house, but an angry mob—fearing that justice might not be done—stormed the place and stoned the detainees to death with roof tiles. For Equitius and Saturninus, these bloody events unfolded on the first day of their tribunician terms (Appian *Civil War* 1.31–32).

In a letter to Atticus dated July 65 B.C., Cicero speculated on the chances of various consular candidates, **Cicero as** including those who might run in 65 or perhaps in the **Political Analyst** following year:

- Publius Sulpicius Galba, praetor in 66. Cicero's comment to Atticus: "A hard worker and tireless campaigner, but one who would have no chance of winning."

- Marcus Caesonius, aedile in 69, praetor in 66. Cicero's comment: "If Caesonius runs, you will want to slap yourself in the forehead!"

- Gaius Aquilius Gallus, praetor in 66. Cicero's comment: "Doubtful; the man has been ill, and prefers to concentrate on his law career."

- Quintus Cornificius, tribune in 69, (possibly) praetor in 66. Cicero's comment: "It seems certain that Cornificius, along with the aforementioned Galba, and Gaius Antonius Hybrida, will all be candidates, news sure to provoke either a smirk or a groan from you."

- Decimus Junius Silanus, possibly aedile in 70 and possibly praetor in 67, and Quintus Minucius Thermus, possibly praetor in 67. Cicero's comment: "Two men whose unpopularity is roughly equivalent to their obscurity."

- Marcus Lollius Palicanus, tribune in 71, and Titus Aufidius, possibly praetor in 67. Cicero's comment: "You certainly do not need me to tell you about these two."

- Lucius Sergius Catilina (Catiline), praetor in 68. Cicero's comment: "As long as the sun shines at noon, Catiline is certain to be a candidate."

- Quintus Curius, possibly praetor in 67. Cicero's comment: "A real darkhorse, who might sneak his name onto the list of candidates."

• Gaius Julius Caesar, aedile in 65. Cicero's comment: "Certain to be a candidate."

Of the eleven politicians Cicero mentioned in his letter, the following actually made it to the consulship: Gaius Antonius Hybrida, in 63; Decimus Junius Silanus, in 62; and Gaius Julius Caesar, in 59 (Cicero *Letters to Atticus*).

Joined at the Hip   One of the unluckiest politicians in all of Roman history had to have been Marcus Calpurnius Bibulus. He held the curule aedileship in 65, the praetorship in 62, and the consulship in 59. Unfortunately, a far more aggressive and prominent politician also held those offices in those years: Gaius Julius Caesar. Caesar consistently outshone Bibulus. During their joint aedileship, for example, Caesar undertook initiatives to decorate the forum and adjacent areas with equipment and materials to be used in the public entertainments he was planning, particularly theatrical productions and mock beast hunts. And even though Bibulus was involved in the planning and financing of these projects, Caesar grabbed the glory all for himself, thus provoking Bibulus to complain, "Just as the temple erected in the Forum to Castor and Pollux bears only the name of Castor, so the joint liberality of Caesar and myself is credited to Caesar alone."

In 62, at the same time that Bibulus was instrumental in helping to crush certain factions of the Catilinarian conspiracy, an armed revolution was masterminded by the dissolute politician Catiline (d. 62 B.C.). Caesar was seeking a higher profile by defending the conspiracy's ringleaders in the senatorial debate over their proper punishment. The Bona Dea scandal, which occurred at Caesar's residence, and his subsequent divorcing of his wife, Pompeia, because of it, also kept Caesar in the public spotlight. (The Bona Dea festival, a women-only secret religious rite, was infiltrated by a man—Publius Clodius—dressed in women's clothing; rumor had it that Clodius was motivated to do so because of the torrid affair in which he and Pompeia were reportedly engaged.)

In 59, this oddest of political odd couples once more found itself in joint tenancy of a major magistracy: the consulship. Once again, Caesar dominated and overshadowed his colleague, to the point that Bibulus did nothing during the last six months of his term of office. He failed even to show up for work, instead staying home and giving as his excuse that the heavenly signs and omens were not favorable for the conduct of public business.

The charade became so ludicrous that people began referring to 59 not as "the year of Bibulus and Caesar," which would have been the standard formula, but as "the year of Julius and Caesar" (Suetonius *Life of Julius Caesar* 10, 20; Dio Cassius 37.41).

When the consul Quintus Fabius Maximus died sud-
denly on December 31 of 45 B.C., a suffect—Gaius Can-   **The Eleventh-**
inius Rebilus—was hastily appointed to fill out the last   **Hour Consul**
few hours of Fabius's term of office. Cicero jokingly com-
mented on this four-hour consulship: "In the consulship of Caninius,
nobody lunched. Still, nothing untoward occurred while he was consul;
for so wonderfully wide awake was he, that during the whole of his
consulship, he never slept!" (Cicero *Letters to His Friends* 7.30; tr. W.
Glynn Williams LCL).

The turbulent political career of Marcus Aemilius
Scaurus summarizes, as well as any politician's career   **A Checkered**
might, the unpredictability of mid–first century B.C. Ro-   **Political Career**
man life.

The wealthy and well-connected Scaurus, stepson of the notorious Lucius Cornelius Sulla, held the quaestorship around 65 B.C. Shortly
thereafter he was sent to Syria to serve as a general. It was not long
before he found an opportunity to increase his already outsized family
fortune.

Two rival local princes had been squabbling for some time over power
and land. When Scaurus arrived in the area, both factions jumped at the
chance to enlist the power of Rome on their side. The more credible offer
seemed to come from Aristobulus (400 talents, a measure of money
equivalent to several million dollars) if Scaurus would support him in
the conflict. Scaurus took the money, gave Aristobulus nominal assistance, and then left—400 talents richer!

A few years later, in 58, he held the office of aedile—and what an
aedilician year it was! Aedile Scaurus sponsored public entertainments
on a vast scale. He imported 150 female leopards and paraded them
through the city streets. He put on display five crocodiles and a hippo-
potamus—a beast never before seen in Rome. He brought from Judaea
the 40-foot-long skeleton of some sort of sea creature and exhibited it in
the city.

The fine arts did not escape Scaurus's notice either. During his aedileship he brought to Rome from Sicyon (near Corinth, in Greece) a number of paintings by the renowned first-century artist Pausias. And he
oversaw what Pliny the Elder called *opus maximum omnium quae umquam
fuere humana manu facta*, "the greatest project of all those which were
ever undertaken by human hands": his theater.

This magnificent theater had an elaborate three-story stage supported
by 360 columns. In the spaces between the columns were 3,000 bronze
statues. The walls of the three stories of the stage were constructed (bottom to top) of marble, hardened glass, and gilded planks; it marked the
first time that marble had ever been used in wall construction in Rome.
The seating area afforded room for 80,000 spectators.

Perhaps most amazing was the fact that the theater was designed to be a merely temporary structure; little more than a month after its construction, it was gone. After the dismantling of the theater, Scaurus whisked away to his Tusculan villa a number of the costumes, set decorations, and other theatrical paraphernalia; the net value of these items was estimated at 30,000,000 sesterces.

Moreover, Scaurus also made off with some of the 360 columns; only the largest (38 feet in length) would do. These he had placed in the halls of his home on the Palatine Hill. As he was transporting the columns, a sewer contractor demanded a security deposit in case the sheer weight of the columns damaged the gutters and substructure of the sewage system.

Scaurus's climb up the political ladder, however, had several rungs yet to go. In the year 56 he took office as one of the praetors; in that capacity he presided over the trial of one Publius Sestius, accused of inciting and participating in street violence. The defendant was represented by (among others) Cicero and was eventually acquitted.

Immediately after his praetorian year, Scaurus went to Sardinia, where he served as provincial governor and also attempted to illegally line his pockets; apparently he still had some overdue bills stemming from his lavish expenditures in 58. In any event, when he returned to Rome in 54 he was prosecuted for provincial improprieties.

The trial was bizarre, even by first-century standards. Scaurus employed no fewer than six defense attorneys, including eminent orators such as Cicero and Quintus Hortensius. Odder still was the presence on the defense team of Publius Clodius Pulcher, perhaps the one man in Rome whom Cicero feared and hated more than any other. Apparently they were able to set aside their differences long enough for the benefit of their beleaguered client.

Additionally, Scaurus enjoyed the active support of nine former consuls, including Pompey the Great, all of whom served primarily as character witnesses. The jurors must have been particularly touched by the testimony of the 94-year-old Marcus Perperna, consul some thirty-eight years earlier in 92.

And Cicero came up with an ingenious (if somewhat racist) argument, one that went something like this: the Sardinians were descended from the Phoenicians (the same forebears of Rome's longtime hated rivals, the Carthaginians). A Phoenician trademark was lying. Therefore, the testimony and evidence offered by the Sardinians must certainly be tainted with untruths.

The strategy worked for Cicero—and for Scaurus. He testified on his own behalf (tearfully, it is said), pointedly recounting for the court his generosity in sponsoring entertainments while he was aedile, and also the noble deeds of his father.

The jury of 70 good men voted 62 to 8 in favor of acquittal. Scaurus was once again free to resume his political machinations; he immediately announced his candidacy for the consulship (of 53) and, following the seemingly accepted campaign tactic of the time, proceeded to offer large bribes to blocks of potential voters. Unfortunately for Scaurus, the same voters had already been bribed by several of the other candidates, so their votes did not register in Scaurus's column on election day.

Because of his attempt to buy the consulship, Scaurus once again found himself in legal hot water and soon was brought to trial. But the impressive list of notables that had jumped to his defense in 54 had dwindled to a precious few in this case. Even Cicero's oratorical magic this time proved ineffective. Scaurus was convicted and sent packing from Rome, a sad ending to a political career that had begun with such promise. (Ancient sources on Scaurus are as follows: Pliny the Elder *Natural History*, especially 36.113–155; Cicero *On Behalf of Scaurus passim*.)

What did the first century B.C. characters Gnaeus Seius, Publius Cornelius Dolabella, Gaius Cassius, and Mark Antony all have in common? A horse, but not just any horse.

A Horse of an Unusual Color

Gnaeus Seius, a clerk of no particular repute, owned an exceedingly handsome and powerful horse bred in Argos, a horse that local legend portrayed as a descendant of the herds belonging to Diomedes of Thrace. Hercules had later spirited the herds away to Argos, or so the story went. The horse in question was a magnificent animal, large and imposing, with a stunning coat and an eyecatching mane.

But the horse had a dark side, too. Anyone who owned him seemed destined to ruin. His first owner, Seius, died a terrible death in the proscriptions of 43 B.C. The next owner, Dolabella, paid the astronomical sum of 100,000 sesterces for the animal; shortly thereafter, Dolabella was killed in Syria, by Romans, during the civil war that broke out after the assassination of Julius Caesar.

Gaius Cassius, the commanding officer of the army that did in Dolabella, had heard of the now-famous horse and claimed him as a spoil of war. Cassius might better have chosen other battlefield souvenirs, for shortly after expropriating the horse he met his own end at the (first) Battle of Philippi.

Mark Antony, vanquisher of Cassius, failed to heed this equine history and became the fourth and final owner. His disgraceful demise in Egypt—whether caused by his possession of the horse or not—is one of Roman history's most noted events.

The curse of the horse of Seius even gave rise to a Roman proverb—

Ille homo habet equum Seianum, "That person has the Seianian horse"—to refer to someone who experienced a calamity or a run of bad luck. (The information about Seius's horse can be found in Aulus Gellius *Attic Nights* 3.9.)

REFERENCES

Appian: *Civil War.*
Aulus Gellius: *Attic Nights.*
Broughton, T.R.S.: *Magistrates of the Roman Republic*, Vol. I.
Dio Cassius: *Roman History.*
Cicero: *Against Verres 2; Letters to Atticus; Letters to His Friends; On Behalf of Scaurus; On the Orator.*
CIL 1.638.
Livy: *From the Founding of the City.*
Pliny the Elder: *Natural History.*
Plutarch: *Life of Cato the Elder; Life of Marius.*
Suetonius: *Life of Julius Caesar.*
Velleius Paterculus: *Compendium of Roman History.*

A pair of gladiators from a wall painting in Pompeii. Notice the heavy protective gear and large shields with which both gladiators are equipped. Reproduced from the Collections of the Library of Congress.

Hunting was a popular pastime. In this illustration, two mounted hunters are closing in on a wild boar. Reproduced from the Collections of the Library of Congress.

A Roman soldier from the time of Julius Caesar. Reproduced from the
Collections of the Library of Congress.

Although meat was probably not a staple of the diets of too many Romans, some ate it occasionally. The illustration shows two men skinning a pig. Reproduced from the Collections of the Library of Congress.

A Roman religious procession, en route to a sacrifice. Reproduced from the Collections of the Library of Congress.

Slaves on display for prospective buyers at an auction. Reproduced from the Collections of the Library of Congress.

Dinner time in a Pompeian home. Reproduced from the Collections of the Library of Congress.

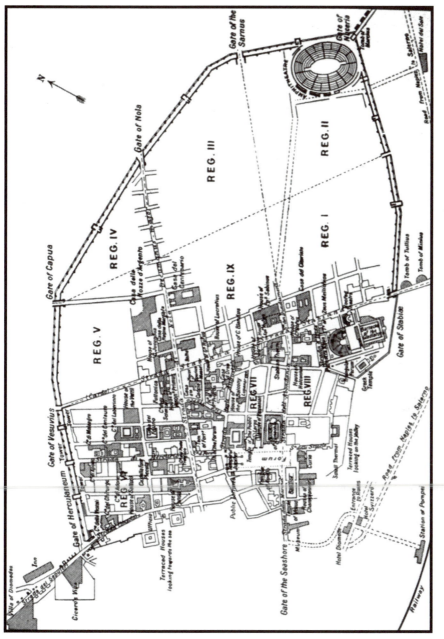

Map of Pompeii. Note the grid form layout of the streets, a standard feature of Roman town planning. The amphitheater (lower right) could accommodate 10,000 spectators, amazing when one considers that the population of Pompeii was roughly 20,000. Reproduced from the Collections of the Library of Congress.

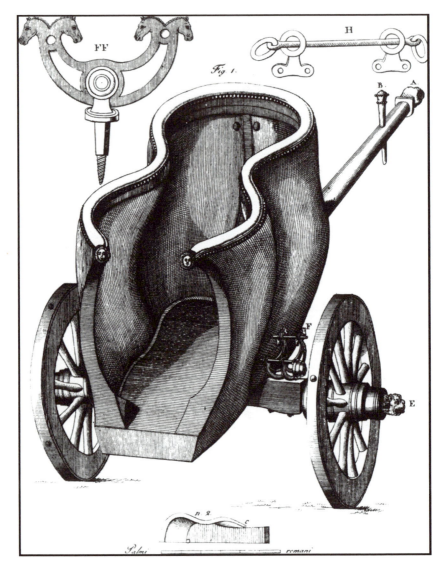

A chariot. Reproduced from the Collections of the Library of Congress.

An idealized land/seascape painting from Pompeii. Reproduced from the Collections of the Library of Congress.

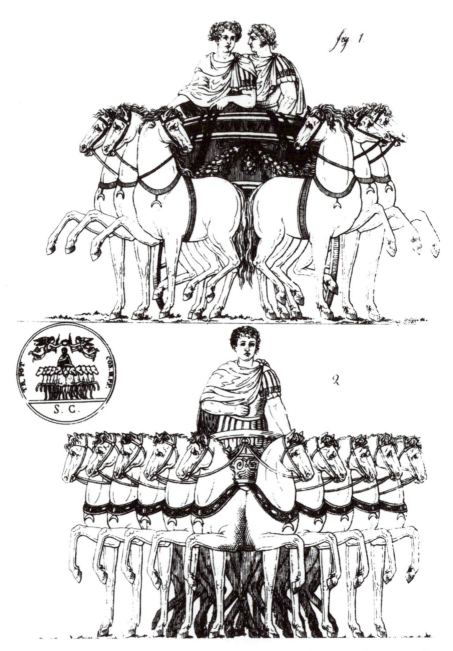

Ceremonial chariots. Chariots used in races were usually drawn by two or four horses, seldom if ever by six or ten, as in the illustrations. Reproduced from the Collections of the Library of Congress.

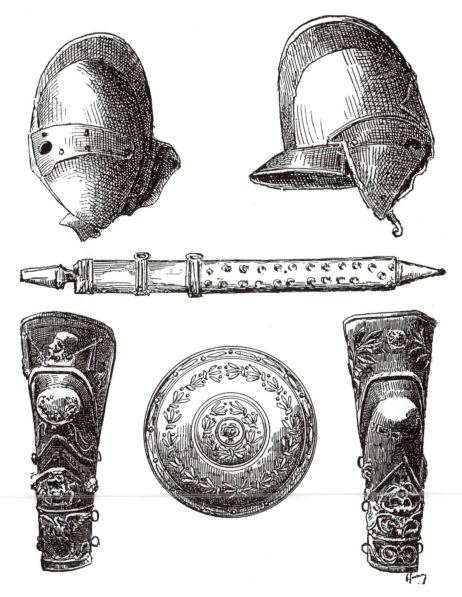

Helmets, sword, shield, and leg protectors used by gladiators. Reproduced from the Collections of the Library of Congress.

The Roman amphitheater in Verona; a scaled-down version of the famous Coliseum in Rome. Reproduced from the Collections of the Library of Congress.

A mosaic floor. Note the prominence of the Medusa figure in the middle of the upper panel. Reproduced from the Collections of the Library of Congress.

A "fast food" restaurant in Pompeii. The rounded forms on top of the wall were actually receptacles for jugs filled with hot or cold liquids. The jugs were stored in the receptacles to help insulate their contents. Reproduced from the Collections of the Library of Congress.

A place for grinding grain. Note the massive size of the millstones. Reproduced from the Collections of the Library of Congress.

Pompeian commerce. The sale of bread (note that bread
loaves were round, like pies). [Note: the captions on the
original say "Naples," but these are all paintings that
were found in Pompeii and later transported to Naples for
display.] Reproduced from the Collections of the Library
of Congress.

Represents the rounded bread loaves, sliced into eight pieces. Reproduced
from the Collection of the Library of Congress.

Typical Pompeian kitchen utensils, the same kinds of baking and cooking implements that one would expect to find in a twenty-first century kitchen. Reproduced from the Collections of the Library of Congress.

Two pensive Pompeians, possibly students or writers. Reproduced from the Collections of the Library of Congress.

Wax tablet from Pompeii. To remove an entry, the wax could be smoothed out with the blunt end of a stylus; the Latin phrase *stilum vertere*, literally "to turn the stylus," means "to erase." Reproduced from the Collections of the Library of Congress.

A dressing room adjacent to the public baths of Stabiae, near Pompeii.
Reproduced from the Collections of the Library of Congress.

Patrons of public baths could select from among a hot bathing pool (*calidarium*), a lukewarm pool (*tepidarium*), or a cold pool (*frigidarium*). Bathers usually frequented all three. Reproduced from the Collections of the Library of Congress.

Coins of Julius Caesar's era. Ancient coins (just as their modern counterparts) were usually engraved with the portrait of a deity or an important personage on one side, and some sort of national symbol on the other. Reproduced from the Collections of the Library of Congress.

The atrium of a well-appointed Pompeian house. A skylight in the ceiling (*impluvium*) admits rainwater, which collects in the receptacle directly beneath (*compluvium*), on the floor. Reproduced from the Collections of the Library of Congress.

Ornate marble tables from a Pompeian house. Reproduced from the Collections of the Library of Congress.

Pompeian homes often included a rectangular open air section surrounded by a colonnaded walkway, with various rooms adjacent to the walkway. In effect, the open portion formed the "backyard" of the house, with the same kinds of features found in modern backyards: bird baths, gardens, lawn furniture, etc. Reproduced from the Collections of the Library of Congress.

Mosaic. Reproduced from the Collections of the Library of Congress.

The statue of a boy found in Pompeii. The stick in his right hand may have been used for some sort of child's game. Reproduced from the Collections of the Library of Congress.

A pricey, multi-storied Pompeian home, with ample space for comfortable living. Despite its immensity, however, it contains many of the features found in smaller, less ornate homes. Examples: *vestibulum* (entry way); *atrium* (first main room, where guests were greeted); *triclinium* (dining room); *porticus* (colonnaded walkway). Reproduced from the Collections of the Library of Congress.

A tutor instructing students. Note the *scrinium*, the round container used for storing scrolls. Reproduced from the Collections of the Library of Congress.

A portrait bust of Seneca. Reproduced from the Collections of the Library of Congress.

Portrait of a Roman (terra cotta). Roman, first
century B.C. Reproduced from the Collections of
the Library of Congress.

Statue of a "Mariage Romain." Reproduced
from the Collections of the Library of
Congress.

A line-drawn reproduction of a bronze bust of a
Pompeian banker, Lucius Caecilius Jucundus.
Reproduced from the Collections of the Library
of Congress.

A Pompeian portrait. Reproduced from the
Collections of the Library of Congress.

7

Family Life

THE ANCIENT ROMANS AT HOME

The phrase "father knows best" has an antiquated chauvinistic ring in these modern times, but in the ancient Roman family the father's rule was law. *Patria potestas*, "the power of the father," gave him virtually unquestioned control over
the affairs of his nuclear family. His children could not marry without his consent; he could even command an adult child to divorce a spouse if he wished. Fathers could, and sometimes did order the exile or even the execution of their adult children. Wives did not enjoy any similar powers; they were generally viewed as subservient to their husbands, as might be expected in such a patriarchal society.

Husbands and Wives

Yet some women established their own identities. In this chapter we will meet some of these women. Cornelia, daughter of the great Scipio Africanus and widow of Tiberius Sempronius Gracchus the Elder, assumed home and family responsibilities normally reserved for the "man of the house," including management of the property and household finances, and the education of the children.

Turia's story is one of wifely devotion to a proscribed husband. A careful reading of the Turia selection can reveal much about a traditional Roman woman's duties, both as a wife and as a mother. Claudia and Horaea, too, were traditional wives; although the ancient sources tell us less about them than we know about Turia, we can still get some idea of the role of Roman wife and mother from their stories.

Women generally had no role in Roman politics. They could not, for example, vote, hold public office or participate in political debate. And they certainly could not function as ambassadors or diplomats. But Vergilia and Volumnia negotiated an end to a destructive fifth-century war, as their story attests.

Sometimes marriages were arranged for political convenience, as the ill-starred marital merger of Mark Antony and Octavia shows. But Octavia had a mind of her own. Marcia, wife of Cato the Younger, was involved in a marriage alliance of a slightly different sort. Finally, Verginia, a young woman who made the supreme sacrifice in a most unconventional manner, is introduced to us in a story that illustrates the absolute power that a father had over his children.

Two Heroic Women. The radical fifth century B.C. patrician Gaius Marcius Coriolanus so hated the political establishment at Rome for compromising with plebeian demands for equality before the law that he was eventually banished from the city. Almost immediately he entered the camp of the Volscians, an intractable enemy of the Romans at the time, and offered them his services as a military leader.

The Volscians put to good use his knowledge of Roman military capabilities; it was not long before Coriolanus, as head of the Volscian army, marched his troops to within 5 miles of Rome, where he established an encampment. Panic spread throughout the city. The Roman senate decided to send a delegation of Coriolanus's friends and (male) family members to him, to appeal to him to end his hostile maneuverings. But he angrily rebuffed them.

Thirty days later a second delegation was sent, with a similar result. And then a third, this time composed of priests. But the holy men were no more successful than their secular counterparts.

Finally a group of Roman matrons decided to take matters into their own hands by appealing to the mother and wife of Coriolanus, Volumnia and Vergilia, respectively. They went to the house of Volumnia, where they found the two women, along with the children of Coriolanus and Vergilia. They urged Volumnia and Vergilia to join them in a direct appeal to Coriolanus to call off what appeared to be an imminent attack on Rome. This the women agreed to do.

When the procession of matrons reached the Volscian camp and Coriolanus recognized his own mother at their head, he was overcome with emotion. He rushed to her and embraced her, and then he hugged his wife. The tears flowed freely.

After he composed himself, he listened as his mother explained the reason for the women's presence. Her speech must have been powerfully effective, for the very next day Coriolanus led his Volscian army out of Roman territory.

When the news of the Volscian retreat reached Rome, rejoicing was unconfined. The Roman senate proclaimed that the women had saved the city; additionally, the senate took the extraordinary step of offering to the women any special privileges they might desire—they need only say the word. Their only request was that a temple to the Fortune of Women be built, and they even volunteered to pay for the structure themselves. The senate decreed that the temple construction begin forthwith, with all expenses to be borne by the state.

In the recent past American culture has been saturated with movies and parties celebrating the toga, the national dress of the ancient Romans. But their closets would contain more than simply togas, and their wardrobe would exhibit nearly as much variety as any but the most obsessive modern-day clothes horse.

Clothing

Lacerna. A loose-fitting cloak that could also be thrown over the head, like a hood.

It's all black and white. Martial (4.2) tells the tale of a certain Horatius, who went to the open-air theater on a chilly day, and hence wore his black *lacerna*; all the other spectators wore white ones. But when snow began falling, it was not long before Horatius's *lacerna*, too, was white.

Watching the skies. Pliny the Elder (18.25) notes that clothing retailers (*vestis institores*) set their prices and inventories according to their best predictions–or guesses of future weather patterns. For example, if they thought that the countryside was due for a wet, chilly winter, they would raise the prices for *lacernae*, just in time for the anticipated demand for winter clothing.

Protect the toga. Sometimes, a *lacerna* might be worn over the toga to protect it, almost like an overcoat. Juvenal (9.28–31) refers to his *pinguis* (thick, heavy) *lacerna* as a *munimenta togae*, a "protector of his toga." Martial also mentions *lacernae* utilized for this purpose (14.135).

Don't leave home with it. Suetonius reports that Augustus was greatly distressed one day when he saw people milling around in the forum wearing dark cloaks and other forms of (what he considered) inappropriate apparel. So he issued a decree that henceforth those who frequented the forum must do so wearing the toga, without cloaks. (Suetonius *Life of Augustus* 40).

Paenula. "A close-fitting, hooded cloak, made of weatherproof material" (OLD).

Let's get ready to rumble! The first century B.C. politician Titus Annius Milo was riding in his wagon (*raeda*) near his home one day, when he was beset by thugs in the employ of his rival, Publius Clodius. Milo met his assailants by jumping down from the wagon, throwing back the *paenula* that he was wearing, and unsheathing his sword. His actions were sufficiently intimidating so as to cause his tormenters to flee. (Cicero *On Behalf of Milo* 29).

Wear it on a trip . . . Martial observes that Roman weather could be fickle and unpredictable, so a traveler should be certain to pack a cloak even on a day that looks to be warm and sunny. At such times, a leather cloak (*paenula scortea*) is the recommended choice, especially as protection against rain. Seneca alludes to the leather *paenula's* protective qualities against hail (Martial 14.130; Seneca *Natural Questions* 4B.6).

. . . but not in court. Tacitus suggests that an orator's effectiveness is reduced if he wears the tight-fitting *paenula* while arguing a case, because the garment restricts his movements, and especially the hand and arm gestures so necessary to an orator's presentation (Tacitus *Dialogue on Oratory* 39).

Clothing Materials. Wool seems to have been the workhorse material for everyday clothing. Apulian wool was particularly well suited for use in cloaks, whereas fleece from northern Italy (in the Po district) was the most expensive, at 100 sesterces per pound.

Pliny the Elder notes the popularity in his own time of a kind of cloak called an *amphimalleum*: one which had both a woolen exterior and a woolen lining. At about the same time, a garment known as a *ventralis* came into vogue, a kind of wool body warmer that could be wrapped around the waist (Pliny the Elder 8.190–193).

Body Decorations. The Romans customarily wore bracelets, necklaces, and armlets, often fabricated from expensive metals. But the most popular form of jewelry was undoubtedly the ring; Pliny the Elder fills in the details:

Pessimum vitae scelus fecit qui primus induit digitis: "Whoever first put [golden rings] on his fingers committed life's most despicable crime." Thus Pliny introduces his discussion of the history of ring-wearing. He notes that in Rome's earliest days, no one seemed to have adorned their fingers in this way; even most of the kings shunned the practice, as did senators and generals.

The practice of wearing rings began in the fourth century B.C. By the time of the Second Punic War (218–201), rings had become common; Hannibal, for example, sent three bushels of Roman rings to Carthage as part of the spoils he collected after the Battle of Cannae (216).

Proliferation followed. Pliny reports that gradually every finger except the middle sported rings, and in some cases, smaller rings for the finger joints were worn. Even slaves began wearing them, although crafted of iron as a sign of their owners' servile status. Even so, slaves sometimes gilded their iron rings.

A small amount of poison was occasionally concealed inside a ring's gemstone. In 52 B.C., some 2,000 pounds of gold kept in Jupiter's temple on the Capitoline mysteriously disappeared. The temple official on whose watch the gold vanished was arrested. But before any legal action could be taken against him, he bit down on his "poisoned" ring, and expired. (Pliny the Elder 33.8 ff)

Tunica. A garment worn under the toga; the men's version was smaller than the women's, ending at the knee, and with short sleeves, while the women's had long sleeves and extended to the feet. The *tunica recta*, a variation of the garment, was worn by brides. The *tunica* *molesta* was treated with pitch and worn by criminals facing execution by fire.

Mackerel Wrappers. Despite the gruesome images connoted by the *tunica molesta*, Martial managed to have some fun with the concept. In one of his epigrams (4.86), he addresses his book of poetry directly, and informs it that to be successful, it must please the sophisticated Apollonius. Otherwise, its pages will be useful only for conversion to *tunicae molestae*, for wrapping not condemned humans, but dead mackerels—for cooking or burying, he does not say.

Catullus (95.8) pokes fun at the historical writings of Volusius by suggesting that they were fit only for use as *laxae tunicae*, "loose tunics" for mackerels.

Short-sleeved tunics only! Aulus Gellius provides a brief history of tunic-wearing in Rome. He states that in Rome's earliest days, men wore togas without tunics; later, they began wearing sleeveless tunics. But they felt that it was inappropriate for a man to wear long-sleeved, full-length tunics, and that only women should dress in such clothing. (Such attire was fitting for women because it provided a seemly covering for their arms and legs.) Long, flowing tunics worn by men were considered a sign of effeminacy, as Publius Africanus, Virgil, and Quintus Ennius all attest (Aulus Gellius 6.12).

Sunday-go-to-meetin'-clothes. The average man in Rome seldom wore a toga (if indeed he even owned one!), except on special occasions. For these people, tunics, not togas, were the national dress, and they were sometimes referenced by the word *tunicati*, "tunic-clad" (Tacitus *Dialogue on Oratory* 7; Horace *Epistle* 1.7).

Synthesis/synthesina. A loose-fitting (often silken) garment, generally worn at dinner parties.

Rich man, poor man. Martial teases a certain Zoilus, who has eleven different sets of dinner clothing, and goes through all eleven at a single party. Why? Ostensibly because the estimable Zoilus sweats so profusely that he would be uncomfortable in a soaked *synthesis*. But Martial suspects that Zoilus merely wishes to show off his wardrobe.

Martial himself, on the other hand, not as ostentatious—or as wealthy—as Zoilus, attends parties with only a single set of dinner clothing (Martial 5.79).

Nero the clothes-horse. The emperor Nero often wore the *synthesis* even when not at dinner, a custom that elicited a fair amount of surreptitious tongue-wagging. He also sported a neckerchief around his neck, as an accessory. Nero's favored *synthesis* was short, and decorated with floral patterns (Suetonius *Life of Nero* 51; Dio 62.13).

Pets The ancient Romans often kept pet animals in their homes. Dogs, of course, were popular household pets, but other creatures also found homes with Roman masters. A wide array of birds—

especially crows, ravens, nightingales, magpies, and sparrows—provided companionship and entertainment, as did various kinds of fish; aviaries and fishponds were fairly commonplace, especially in the homes or the estates of wealthy Romans. Cats, oddly, were less common as household pets and seem to have been regarded as valuable more for rodent control than for companionship.

One of the most famous pet animals in Roman literature was Sertorius's white fawn. His story follows.

Sertorius and the White Fawn. Quintus Sertorius, a first century B.C. governor of Spain, conjured up a number of tricks to retain the loyalty and obedience of his troops and also of the native peoples. He used a pet fawn in that way.

A certain Spanus, who lived in the countryside close to the Roman encampment, happened across a doe that had recently given birth and was evidently fleeing hunters. Spanus could not capture the doe, but he did manage to catch her fawn, a remarkable animal because it was pure white from nose to tail. Spanus brought it to Sertorius's headquarters and gave it to him.

At first Sertorius regarded the gift only as a trifle, and one that he would probably soon set free. But the fawn quickly became very tame and followed Sertorius wherever he went. So he began to think of ways in which he might exploit the situation to his own advantage.

Finally he hit upon this scheme: he would claim that the fawn was a gift of the goddess Diana and, moreover, that he could communicate with it and that it had shared many secrets with him. He imparted added credibility to the claim by naming the fawn as his informant on military invasions and outcomes of battles (when in reality he had received that information from human agents).

His trickery worked, for everyone who saw Sertorius and his famous white fawn believed that the animal truly was sacred and that Sertorius must therefore be specially favored by the gods (Plutarch *Life of Sertorius* 11).

A Real Dogfight. During the course of Trimalchio's banquet (a lavish bash described in Petronius' *Satyricon*, first century A.D.), a fight broke out between two of the household's pet dogs: a behemoth of a mutt named Scylax, and a little lap dog named Pearl. Petronius describes the chaotic scene:

[Trimalchio's favorite slave Croesus] was tying up an unnaturally obese black puppy in a green handkerchief, and then putting a broken piece of bread on a chair, and cramming it down the throat of the dog, who did not want it and felt sick. . . . Trimalchio . . . ordered them to bring in Scylax, "the guardian of the house and the slaves." An enormous dog on a chain was at once led in, and on receiving a kick from the porter as a hint to lie down, he curled up in front of the table. Then Trimalchio threw him a bit of white bread and said, "No one in my house loves me better than Scylax." The favorite put down the puppy and encouraged her to attack at once. Scylax, after the manner of dogs, of course, filled the dining-room with a most hideous barking, and nearly tore Croesus' little Pearl to pieces. And the uproar did not end with a dog-fight, for a lamp upset over the table, and broke all the crystal to pieces, and sprinkled some of the guests with hot oil. (Petronius *Satyricon* 64; tr. Michael Hesseltine LCL)

Canine Mood Swings. The poet Lucretius (ca. 99 B.C.–ca. 55) notes that Molossian hounds—a fearsome dog breed—show their fangs, growl, and bark menacingly when they are threatened or agitated. But these same dogs, when tending to their puppies, somehow metamorphose into docile and gentle creatures, licking their pups, playfully batting them with their paws, pretending to snap at them, and even occasionally half-swallowing their tiny bodies (Lucretius 5.1062–1072).

Pet Dolphins. Pliny the Elder relates the story of a tame dolphin living in Lake Lucrinus during the reign of Augustus (ruled 27 B.C.–A.D. 14). This creature took a liking to a youngster who resided in the region. At midday the boy would go to the lakeshore and feed the dolphin pieces of bread; he called him Simon, or Snubnose in English. In fact, any time that the boy visited the lake, he had only to call out the dolphin's name, and Snubnose would rise from the depths. He used to eat from his young friend's hand and even ferried him about the lake on his back. The boy's school was located on the lake's opposite shore; he often rode there on the dolphin in the morning and enjoyed a return trip after the school day was over.

This method of transport continued for several years until the boy contracted some unspecified childhood disease and died. Nonetheless the loyal Snubnose continued to swim to the place where he and the boy customarily met—almost like a mourner, according to Pliny—until the dolphin, too, eventually breathed his last.

Pliny also relates a tale about a tame dolphin living in the Mediterranean Sea near Hippo Diarrhytus, a town in northern Africa. This dolphin used to accept food from people's hands and submit to petting and stroking. It would also frolic with swimmers and give them rides on its back. Eventually, however, the residents of Hippo Diarrhytus killed it, because their small town could not accommodate the officials and others who traveled there to see the dolphin (Pliny the Elder *Natural History* 9.25–27).

ROMAN NAMES

Many Roman men of high esteem, like their modern counterparts, possessed a tripartite name. The three components were labeled *praenomen*, *nomen*, and *cognomen*.

The *praenomen*, equivalent to a modern first name, was limited in its variety. Only about sixteen were used:

Aulus	Marcus	Servius
Appius	Manius	Sextus
Gaius	Numerius	Spurius
Gnaeus	Publius	Titus
Decimus	Quintus	Tiberius
Lucius		

Economy of numbers bestowed such a general familiarity upon these names that they were almost never written in full. First-letter abbreviations were the norm, except in the cases of Appius, Gnaeus, and Tiberius: Ap., Gn., and Ti., respectively, distinguished them from the A., G., and T. of Aulus, Gaius, and Tiberius. Manius generally appeared as M', with the unadorned M. reserved for Marcus.

The second component, the *nomen* (*gens*, or family name) was probably the most important, if for no other reason than that it distinguished patricians from plebeians. Noted patrician *nomina* included Julius, Cornelius, Aemilius, Claudius, and Marcius. Some plebeian examples included Octavius, Sempronius, and Junius.

The third name, the *cognomen*, indicated a specific branch of a particular family. *Cognomina* were often awarded as honorary epithets or as descriptors of physical characteristics. However, instances abound of recipients of these nicknames passing them along to their offspring, so that the event that prompted them became less prominent with the passage of time.

Other honorary *cognomina* could be added—technically called *agnomina*—resulting in four- or even five-part names.

Cognomina with Stories Attached   *Fear This, Porsenna!* In the late sixth century B.C., when Rome was under siege by the Etruscan king Lars Porsenna, a young man named Gaius Mucius stepped forward with a plan: he would swim across the Tiber River in the dead of night, infiltrate the Etruscan camp, and attempt to assassinate Porsenna.

The scheme backfired when the Etruscan guards seized Mucius at a critical moment and brought him into the king's presence. During the inevitable interrogation, the young Roman—to demonstrate his courage and his indifference to pain—thrust his right fist into a nearby sacrificial fire. Porsenna was so impressed that he released Mucius, who was thereafter known as Gaius Mucius Scaevola, the cognomen meaning "left-handed man."

A Weed-Free Farm. Gaius Licinius Stolo was undoubtedly more famous for his forays into politics than for his farming pursuits; in 367 B.C. he introduced and passed legislation limiting the size of farms and ranches to 500 *iugera* (a little over 300 acres). But his own farm was so scrupulously cultivated that the trees on it never suffered the indignities of weedy-appearing shoots, *stolones*, surrounding the bases of their trunks (Varro *On Agriculture* 1.2.).

Something to Chew On. Manius Curius, consul in 290, 275, and 274 B.C., received the cognomen Dentatus ("Toothy") because he was born with a full set of teeth (Pliny the Elder 7.68).

They Were the Greatest. The Fabius Maximus family produced a number of noted politicians and military leaders. Plutarch relates stories about the origins of both names. First, Fabius: family members were originally named Fodius (pl. Fodii) because they were noted hunters, especially skilled in trapping animals in camouflaged holes or pits. The name Fodius, so it was said, derived from the Latin words *fossas fodere*, "to dig ditches."

Quintus Fabius Maximus, the Roman dictator in 216 B.C. and nemesis of Hannibal, had the agnomen Verrucosus, "Little Wart," because he had a small, wartlike growth on his upper lip (Plutarch *Life of Fabius Maximus* 1).

Pig Mongery. Publius Cornelius Scipio Nasica Serapio, consul in 138 B.C., was perhaps best known for a dubious claim to fame: he led the uprising in 133 that resulted in the violent death of his cousin, the crusading reformer Tiberius Sempronius Gracchus.

He apparently received the agnomen Serapio during his consulship. It was jeeringly bestowed upon him by a tribune, Gaius Curiatus, who thought that he bore a resemblance to a pig dealer bearing the same name (Pliny the Elder *Natural History* 7.54: 21.10; Livy *From the Founding of the City* 55).

A Weighty Matter. One of the consuls for 137 B.C., Marcus Aemilius Lepidus, found it difficult to perform his military duties because of extreme obesity and a concomitant inability to engage in physical activities. Hence he "earned" the agnomen Porcina, a Latin word translatable as "Porky" (Diodorus Siculus *Library of History* 33.27).

Even in Ancient Rome, Some Men Were Pigs. Gnaeus Tremellius Scrofa, considered by Varro the *de agricultura Romanus peritissimus*—"the Roman most knowledgeable about farming"—bore the appropriate (or inappropriate?) cognomen Scrofa, meaning "sow." According to Varro (*On Agriculture* 2.4), the estimable Gnaeus explained the origin of the name thus:

His grandfather, Lucius Tremellius, was the first man in his family to sport the swinish nickname. Lucius had been given temporary command of the Roman army in the province of Macedonia around the year 136 B.C. The hostile Macedonians viewed this as a golden opportunity to win

a victory against a general whom they apparently viewed as inexperi-
enced, so they attacked.

When Lucius saw the assault unfolding, he rallied his soldiers to arms,
vowing that the Romans would disperse the attackers in a manner reminiscent of a sow putting her piglets to flight. And the skirmish played
out precisely as Lucius predicted. Afterward, Lucius Tremellius received
the cognomen Scrofa. All his descendants inherited the name, including
Gnaeus Tremellius, the agricultural expert. Not surprisingly, Gnaeus's
particular area of expertise was swineherding.

On the other hand, Macrobius (*Saturnalia* 1.6) provides a less noble
account of the name: Lucius Tremellius's slaves had stolen a sow from
a neighboring farm and slaughtered the unfortunate animal; they subsequently concealed the carcass under the bed of Tremellius's wife.
When the angry neighbor later appeared and demanded to be allowed
to search the house, Tremellius claimed that the only sow he had on the
premises was the two-legged one who doubled as his wife!

The Chickpea. Marcus Tullius's cognomen, Cicero ("Chickpea"), was
first conferred upon some ancestor of his who had an indentation at the
tip of his nose; the nasal notch apparently resembled a chickpea. Even
though this earliest Cicero was sometimes ridiculed for his cognomen,
he and his descendants grew attached to it and retained it as part of the
family name.

When Marcus Tullius Cicero (the first-century orator) first became involved in politics, some of his friends advised him to change the cognomen or discard it altogether. Cicero firmly rejected such suggestions,
saying that he would make his third name more famous and respected
than those of other notable Romans, such as Scaurus ("Gouty") or Catulus ("Puppy Dog").

Later, while serving as quaestor in Sicily (75 B.C.), he made a dedica-
tion of a silver plate on which he had ordered to be engraved the names
Marcus and Tullius, followed by a representation of a chickpea (Plutarch
Life of Cicero 1).

A Politician with a Leg Up. Publius Cornelius Lentulus Sura had an
up-and-down political career. Praetor in 74 B.C. and consul in 71, he was
expelled from the Roman senate in 70 for various improprieties; later he
rose from the ashes to become praetor again, in 63, whereupon he became mixed up with the Catilinarian conspiracy, an armed revolution
masterminded by the dissolute politician Catiline (d. 62 B.C.) Eventually
he resigned his praetorship and was ultimately executed for his role in
the plot.

But earlier in his career (in 81) Lentulus held the quaestorship, at
which time he was accused of inappropriately administering public
funds. When he was called before the senate to explain himself, he oozed
flippancy and snidely remarked that the senate could have his leg, "give

'em a leg" evidently being a saying drawn from Roman playgrounds and used by children to refer to a missed catch during games of ball.

The reference stuck. *Sura* is Latin for "leg"; and after this incident in the senate, the rascally senator was known as Publius Cornelius Lentulus Sura, "The Leg" (Plutarch *Life of Cicero* 17).

HOW ITALY GOT ITS NAME

There are at least two stories about the origin of the name "Italy," and thanks to Dionysius of Halicarnassus, we possess accounts of both.

According to one of these stories, Italy was named for one of its early rulers, a certain Italus, a wise and prudent leader. At the beginning of his reign he held sway over only the southern tip of the Italian peninsula, but gradually he extended his district's boundaries until he ruled a good many cities. So widely was his influence felt that the whole area under his dominion was eventually named after him.

Hercules figures prominently in the other story. Hercules was engaged in herding Geryon's cattle from the island of Erythia, near Spain, to Argos, via the region now known as Italy, when one of the calves escaped. The animal wandered down the Italian coast to the southernmost portion of the peninsula, whereupon it swam across the straits to Sicily.

Hercules tracked the calf all the way to the island, inquiring of the inhabitants as he went if anyone had seen the stray. Unfortunately a language barrier made this difficult, because the people of Italy and Sicily did not speak Greek, and Hercules spoke nothing but Greek. Eventually, however, he was able to make himself understood, and they, in turn, used the Latin word for calf—*vitulus*—when conversing with him about it.

Whether Hercules ever found the animal, Dionysius does not say; but he does inform us that Hercules named the lands he had traversed "Vitulia," to commemorate the hunt. Dionysius concludes the anecdote by remarking that "it is no wonder that the name has been [slightly] changed in the course of time to its present form, since many Greek names, too, have met with a similar fate" (Dionysius of Halicarnassus *Roman Antiquities* 1.35).

REFERENCES

Aulus Gellius: *Attic Nights.*
Cicero: *On Behalf of Milo.*
Dio Cassius: *Roman History.*
Diodorus Siculus: *Library of History.*
Dionysius of Halicarnassus: *Roman Antiquities.*
Horace: *Epistle.*

Livy: *From the Founding of the City.*
Lucretius: *On the Nature of Things.*
Macrobius: *Saturnalia.*
Martial: *Epigrams.*
Petronius: *Satyricon.*
Pliny the Elder: *Natural History.*
Plutarch: *Life of: Cicero; Fabius Maximus; Sertorius.*
Seneca: *Natural Questions.*
Suetonius: *Life of: Augustus; Nero.*
Tacitus: *Dialogue on Oratory.*
Varro: *On Agriculture.*

8

Holidays and Leisure Activities

ROMAN FESTIVALS

The ancient Romans enjoyed many of the same kinds of leisure activities that attract devotees in modern cultures: fishing, swimming, various games played with balls, board and dice games, running, or perhaps simply going for walks. But in addition to these somewhat informal activities, a number of organized public festivals, or *feriae*, dotted the Roman calendar. These *feriae* were originally intended to honor the gods, but many (if not most) took on a singularly secular character.

One of the most famous *feriae* was the Saturnalian festival, celebrated annually from December 17 to December 23, in honor of the god Saturn. The Saturnalia was one **Io Saturnalia!** of the oldest (founded in the early fifth century B.C., according to Livy [*From the Founding of the City* 2.21]) and most popular Roman festivals; that it was held around the time of the winter solstice was probably not a coincidence.

It was a time of general merrymaking in which children were freed from their studies; and business, commerce, and the legal machinery of the city ground to a halt.

During the Saturnalia—and particularly on the first day—revelers would shout the exclamation *"Io Saturnalia!"* in the course of their partying. In a poem published during the Saturnalia of A.D. 96, Martial gleefully writes that the stern and somber strictures of overly serious figures must be gone during the festival: *Ite foras!* ("Get out of here!"). Let the celebration begin . . . *Io Saturnalia!* (Martial *Epigrams* 11.2).

Cicero offers an account of Julius Caesar's observance of the Saturnalian festival for 45 B.C. On December 19, according to Cicero, Caesar arrived at the seacoast town of Puteoli. He went for a short walk along the seashore, following that with a bath and a massage. Then he appeared at dinner, where he ate and drank with unbounded joy. Many partygoers were present, including Cicero himself; he describes the evening as one of pleasant camaraderie, with no "shoptalk" (probably a reference to the current political climate) but with much discussion of literary topics (Cicero *Letters to Atticus* 13.52).

Even the habitually frugal Cato the Elder (234–149 B.C.) recognized that the Saturnalian festival was special: he prescribed for his farmhands an additional $3\frac{1}{2}$ *congii* (about 20 pints) of wine per man during the festal period (Cato the Elder *On Agriculture* 57).

Seneca (4 B.C.–A.D. 65) grumpily remarks that the whole citizenry sweats in December. How is this possible, in such a chilly month? Because everyone is either preparing to celebrate or actually celebrating the Saturnalia—and doing so with great gusto. Seneca seemed to dislike this and other holidays, not so much because of the festivities but because of the excesses in which many of his fellow Romans indulged: "It shows much more courage to remain dry and sober when the mob is drunk and vomiting"; a person should be able to celebrate holidays without going overboard (Seneca *Moral Epistles* 18; tr. Richard Gummere LCL).

When Pliny the younger (A.D. 62–112) visited his Laurentian villa in December, he preferred to study, not party. But scholarly pursuits were impossible because of the noise produced by his celebrating household. So, to escape the cacophony, Pliny customarily secluded himself in a wing of the house called the *diaeta*, a sort of annex separated from the main part of the house by a wall and a garden. Here, in his quasi-soundproofed retreat, the studious Pliny could read and write to his heart's content and not be bothered by the party animals in the other parts of the house (Pliny the Younger *Natural History* 2.17).

Gladiatorial Shows. Statius poetically described how the Saturnalia was celebrated in conjunction with a gladiatorial show sometime during the reign of the emperor Domitian (A.D. 81–96). All sorts of edible goodies were distributed to the spectators: biscuits, pastries, cakes, dates, and assorted fruits. Some attendees brought their own food and wine, carry-in style, in picnic baskets. Statius alluded to the egalitarian nature of the festival when he mentioned that members of every social class rubbed elbows at the Saturnalian games: *libertas reverentiam remisit*, "the freedom [afforded by the Saturnalia] has sent class distinctions packing." Even the poorest of the poor could, on this one occasion, claim to be the personal guests of the emperor.

Strange sights were also seen on the arena floor: women gladiators battling each other, and then a company of dwarfs who fought as fiercely as the most aggressive professional gladiators.

The fun had hardly begun when night began to fall; the darkness ushered in music, applause, and exotic dancing girls. At about the same time, a flock of flamingos and pheasants descended on the arena. And after that? "Who can sing of the spectacle, the unrestrained mirth, the banqueting, the unbought feast [i.e., provided at no charge], the lavish streams of wine? . . . For how many years shall this festival abide? Never shall age destroy so holy a day!" (Statius *Forests* 1.6; tr. J. H. Mozley LCL).

The Lupercalian festival, a fertility rite, held annually on February 15, was reminiscent of modern winter carnivals often celebrated in January or February in northern cities. The festival featured partying, **The Lupercalian Festival** drinking, and—its most bizarre aspect—young men running about the Palatine Hill clad only in leather loincloths and brandishing whips. These Luperci, as they were called, lashed any women they encountered, supposedly to ensure fertility. Perhaps the most (in)famous of these Luperci was Mark Antony.

During the Lupercalian festival for 44 B.C., a well-sloshed Mark Antony—presumably after completing a lap or two around the Hill—approached Julius Caesar and attempted to place a crown on the latter's head. Or, as Cicero deftly worded it, "you ought not to have thought Marcus Antonius a consul after the Lupercalia. . . . Before the eyes of the Roman people, he harangued while naked, anointed, and drunk, and aimed at placing a diadem on his colleague's [Caesar's] head." Caesar, not wishing to convey even the appearance of aspiring to royalty, refused to accept Antony's "gift," but many observers nonetheless reached that conclusion; this "crowning" incident was likely a factor in Caesar's assassination on the Ides of March, a mere one month after the Antonian frolic (Cicero *Philippics* 3.12; tr. Walter C. A. Ker LCL; Suetonius *Life of Julius Caesar* 79).

The Romans observed April 21 as the date of their city's founding (in the year 753 B.C.) and celebrated it in a festival called the Parilia. (The Parilia was origi- **The Parilia (Founding Day)** nally an agrarian festival that eventually merged into the founding day observance.) Propertius (ca. 50–ca. 16 B.C.) noted that the day was celebrated with feasting, partying, and this odd twist: the burning of hay bales, which the drunken revelers tried to leap over without getting scorched (Propertius *Elegies* 4.4).

The Ludi Romani (Roman Games)
Some annual festivals emphasized chariot and horse races; the most famous of these was probably the Ludi Romani, or Roman Games, celebrated each year from September 4 to 19. Dionysius of Halicarnassus (late first century B.C.) provides the details. The games were preceded, he says, by a huge parade whose route stretched from the Capitoline Hill, through the forum, all the way to the Circus Maximus. The parade participants included (in the order indicated):

1. young Roman men on horseback, men who came from distinguished families and had almost attained the age of manhood

2. young Roman men on foot, from less notable households

3. charioteers, some driving four-horse chariots, others driving two-horse chariots, still others riding unyoked horses

4. athletes who would compete in what Dionysius calls "the light and heavy games," probably footraces and combat events (boxing, wrestling), respectively

5. numerous groups of armed dancers composed of men, teenagers, and young boys, along with flutists and lyre players; the dancers wore plumed helmets and carried swords and spears

6. men dressed like satyrs (woodland deities), wearing shaggy clothing made of animal skins and decked out with a variety of garden flowers

7. a second group of flutists and lyre players, followed by incense bearers and men carrying various kinds of jugs made of gold or silver

8. the last parade members: images of the gods (several dozen were represented) carried by men on their shoulders

After the parade the consuls and select priests conducted animal sacrifices (oxen); then, finally, the games themselves unfolded: horse races and several kinds of chariot races, including contests involving two-, three-, and four-horse chariots. Next came footraces and boxing and wrestling matches (Dionysius of Halicarnassus *Roman Antiquities* 7.72).

Too Hot. In *Letters to His Brother Quintus* (3.1), Cicero mentions that he skipped the Ludi Romani for 54 B.C.; the September heat was too stifling, so Cicero instead went home to Arpinum, where, he said, he whiled away the hours enjoying the view, and especially the Fibrenus River.

A Hefty Price Tag. The Ludi Romani of 217 B.C. cost a whopping 333,333 1/3 bronze *asses*, not to mention the sacrifice of 300 oxen to Jupiter, as well as similar sacrifices to a number of other gods (Livy *From the Founding of the City* 22.10).

In the days of Camillus (early fourth century B.C.),
the Romans often found themselves threatened by
neighboring tribes. One of these, the Latins, sent a
messenger to Rome demanding free-born young
women for them to marry. The Roman authorities did
not quite know how to interpret this ultimatum. On the one hand, they
thought that perhaps the Latins made the demand in order to establish
marriage ties between themselves and the Romans. It seemed more
likely, however, that the women, if handed over, would be used as little
more than hostages. And if the Romans refused to comply, war would
be the likely consequence.

**The Capratine
Nones Honor the
"Night Light"**

In the midst of this uncertainty, a young servant woman named Tutula
stepped forward. She had a plan. She suggested to the Roman magistrates that they send her, along with a contingent of the most attractive
maidservants, to the Latin camp; they would all be dressed and made
up to appear to be free-born women. Then, after an evening of partying
and drinking, and after the Latin soldiers had drifted off to sleep, the
women would remove and hide all the soldiers' weaponry, and the Romans could then launch a night assault on the Latin encampment. The
magistrates gave their approval to Tutula's scheme.

It worked perfectly. The unsuspecting Latins accepted the women, the
evening's activities unfolded as planned, and the swords and other
weapons were whisked away from the slumbering soldiers. At that point
Tutula climbed to the top of a tall fig tree and lit a torch that was visible
in Rome; this was the signal that the coast was clear. The Roman soldiers
advanced and easily captured the camp.

The Romans subsequently held an annual festival to commemorate
this event (on the Nones of July, or July 5, a festival quite similar to
modern re-enactments of famous historical battles). The men would run
forth from the city gates calling loudly to each other, as though they
were soldiers rushing to battle. The women then would join in, joking
with and taunting the men as they ran. After a mock battle between the
men and the women, they would all retire to the shade of nearby trees
to enjoy a picnic lunch.

The festal day was subsequently called the Capratine Nones, from *ca-
prificus*, the Latin word for wild fig tree, the kind of tree Tutula had
climbed to display her "night light" signal (Plutarch *Life of Camillus* 33).

BIRTHDAYS

A Roman birthday celebration was surprisingly similar to its modern
counterpart. The big day featured gatherings of family members and
friends, with gift giving and banqueting forming a major part of the

celebration. The ancient Roman version of a birthday card—the *geneth-liacon*, or birthday poem—was sometimes sent to or recited for the celebrant. Examples of birthday poems written by Ausonius, Ovid, and Tibullus follow.

Sweet Sixteen The fourth century A.D. writer and teacher Ausonius composed a poem for his grandson—also named Ausonius—on the event of the boy's sixteenth birthday. A modern paraphrase might go like this:

When you were still a young child, and first learning to read and write. I did not add my own two sesterces' worth to the lessons your own teacher had prepared for you. I did not want to do anything that might discourage you from developing a love for those studies. And now that you are almost a man, and able to make your own choices in life, I offer you my prayers and best wishes.

As you know, I recently suffered a near-fatal illness, and I thank the gods that they spared me so that I could live to see you celebrate this milestone. It has been and it is a special joy for me to watch my grandson grow, mature, and now stand at the threshold of manhood.

Sixteen years ago, on the Ides [13th] of September, you were born. An auspicious day, the Ides. You probably know that Hecate, Mercury, and Vergil drew their first breaths on the Ides of August, May, and October. (Ausonius *Epistles* 21)

A Birthday in Exile Ovid (43 B.C.–A.D. 17) wrote a poem on the occasion of his birthday—he does not tell us the date or his age—while he was in exile in Tomis. The tone and content of the poem show that his birthday was hardly a happy one. The highlights of the poem, addressed to his *genius natalis*, "birthday god," are as follows:

Another birthday! What's the point? It only marks yet another year away from home and family. Why did you not do your best to see to it that your final visit to me in Italy really *was* your final visit to me?

Why did you follow me out here, to this freezing cold place that all the gods have forsaken? I suppose you think I'm going to celebrate, is that it? Get out the white robe, burn a little incense on the altar, bake myself a birthday cake, and wish myself many happy returns?

No way! I'd rather see a funeral altar! In fact, here's my wish, birthday god, the best present you could give: don't come around here next year at this time! (Ovid *Tristia* 3.13)

Ovid also wrote a poem in honor of his wife's birthday. The sentiments go something like this:

Another year has zipped by, and here I am, just like Odysseus, spending my wife's birthday with my wife in absentia. I only dig out the birthday celebratory stuff once a year, so I might as well get to it. The white robe, the grass-covered altar, a garland or two, a little incense.

I only hope that she is happier than I am today, that she is safe at home with our daughter, and even though I am not there to celebrate with her, I pray that everything else in her life goes well. Many happy returns to her, and many more birthdays!

Things surely turned out differently than I expected. Who would have thought that I would be observing my wife's birthday alone here in the middle of nowhere, among barbarian tribes? Ah, but the smoke from the incense. . . . It rises into the air and drifts to the west, toward Italy, as if it had a mind of its own. At least the smoke can escape this cheerless place.

There must be a silver lining to our clouds of misery. Maybe it is this: just as Odysseus's long and painful separation from Penelope brought fame to her by her fidelity to him; just as Alcestis gained renown because of her willingness to die in place of her husband, Admetus; just as Laodamia carved out a niche for herself in Greek legend by virtue of her undying love for her husband, Protesilaus [first Greek to die in the Trojan War], perhaps my wife as well, through the sufferings of her husband, will gain a measure of immortality.

I pray that Augustus will spare my grieving wife, who deserves better than that which fate has pushed upon her. (*Tristia* 5.5)

Cornutus received a poetic birthday greeting from his friend Tibullus, the first century B.C. poet. Tibullus expounds on his birthday wishes for Cornutus: that an altar may be fragrant with the smell of burning incense; that there may be garlands for his head, and plenty of honey **Birthday Greetings to Cornutus** cakes to eat, and wine to drink. And that whatever Cornutus wishes for, he may get.

Tibullus knows his friend well enough to realize that he prefers the love of his wife to all the world's well-tilled fields and all the pearls that come from the East. So that is the poet's birthday wish for Cornutus: that he may enjoy married life up to ripe old age and that the gods will bless him and his wife with a brood of happy children (Tibullus 2.2).

When the poet Martial (ca. A.D. 40–ca. 104) tried to give a birthday present to his friend Quintus, the latter **No Gifts, Please** refused to accept it. So Martial suggested a course of action that would please both of them: Quintus could give Martial a gift (Martial *Epigrams* 9.53).

LEISURE ACTIVITIES

Life Jackets. Novice swimmers apparently used the ancient equivalent of water wings to help them stay afloat as **Swimming** they attempted to learn to swim. Horace's (65–8 B.C.) father admonished his son that when he was still a child, the father could protect him from life's misfortunes; but once he had come of age, he would have to be responsible for himself, like a young swimmer learning to keep his head above water "without cork." Plautus (ca. 255–184 B.C.) refers to reed or bamboo floats, which enabled the wearer to learn to use his arms properly while not tiring himself out merely trying to stay buoyant (Horace *Satires* 1.4; Plautus *Pot of Gold* 595).

What Hebrus Does for Fun. The poet Horace described a certain Hebrus who was so expert a swimmer that he could successfully negotiate the strong currents of the Tiber River. In addition, he was an expert boxer and a fast runner, undefeated in those events, according to Horace. When not swimming, boxing, or running, Hebrus liked to hunt. He often brought home a deer or two, or perhaps a wild boar (Horace *Odes* 3.12).

Another Tiber Swimmer. A certain Enipeus was noted for his ability to swim down the middle of the Tiber; no one could do it faster (Horace *Odes* 3.7).

Taking a Dive. One of the most celebrated semi-legendary figures in early Roman history, Horatius Cocles, was in charge of guarding the Sulpician Bridge one night when he noticed a large band of Etruscan soldiers heading his way with hostile intent. The other Romans fled the scene, but Horatius remained to face the onslaught alone. He kept the Etruscans at bay until the bridge collapsed (its pilings having been intentionally weakened by a small cadre of Romans beneath), whereupon Horatius plunged into the Tiber River, still fully outfitted in his suit of armor.

Thus encumbered, with spears and arrows falling all around him, he managed to evade all the missiles as he swam to safety on the opposite shore (Livy *From the Founding of the City* 2.10ff).

Swim for Your Life! The emperor Nero (ruled A.D. 54–68) suffered from a noteworthy deficiency in the mother-son relationship: he hated Agrippina, his mother, and for some time had plotted to kill her. But how? Poison, perhaps. But he eliminated this method for matricide, because Agrippina was a cautious woman, always on the alert for attempts on her life. Besides, she had strengthened and fortified her body by habitually consuming antidotes to commonly used poisons. On the other hand, running her through with a sword or a dagger would be messy and difficult to cover up. A different course of action had to be devised.

The freedman Anicetus devised a brilliant scheme (Anicetus detested Agrippina, and the feeling was mutual). He suggested to Nero that it would be possible to construct a collapsible boat that could fall apart when out to sea, with the inevitable drowning of any passengers. The beauty of the plan lay in its foolproof nature: no one would be able to prove that the boat was designed to disintegrate or that murder most foul had been intended.

And the timing was perfect. Nero had planned to celebrate the festival of Minerva (held in March) in the fashionable resort town of Baiae. He invited his mother to join him there for the festivities. Although reluctant, she agreed. The banqueting lasted far into the night, whereupon Nero suggested to his mother that she might want to take a boat ride to Bauli, a nearby villa where she would spend the night.

So Agrippina and two servants (Crepereius Gallus and Acerronia), as well as other passengers, boarded the ill-fated boat. Not long after departure, the craft began to break apart; Nero's devious plan seemed to be working to perfection. Crepereius was instantly killed by falling debris; Acerronia, hoping to save herself amid the chaos by identifying herself as Agrippina, was immediately set upon by the conspiratorial crew and beaten to death.

But the real Agrippina managed to elude the murderers and slip into the water, whereupon she began frantically swimming to shore. Fortunately (for her, if not Nero!), she was soon plucked from the brine by the crew of a fishing boat in the area and thus transported safely to shore.

A footnote: Nero finally sent some assassins to kill his mother—which they did—and he then tried to explain her demise as a suicide. Sources for this anecdote are as follows: Tacitus *Annals* 14.3–7; Suetonius *Life of Nero* 34.

The Ink Stayed Dry. Julius Caesar (100–44 B.C.) numbered swimming among his many talents. On one occasion he accompanied a party of soldiers assaulting a bridge in Alexandria. Having been turned back by the bridge's defenders, he leapt over the side into an already crowded dingy. Seeing that the small boat could not accommodate another passenger, he dove into the water and swam some 200 yards to the nearest Roman ship—all the while dragging his heavy cloak by his teeth and holding aloft in his left hand some important papers that he did not want to get wet (Suetonius *Life of Julius Caesar* 64).

Swimming Like a Rock. A more laughably pathetic swimmer was Vergil's Menoetes, a ship's captain who took his dip quite unwillingly. It happened during a boat race described in Book V of the *Aeneid* (ca. 1200 B.C.) Four craft were involved in the contest; their object was to set out from shore, row to a small, rocky island some way out to sea, circle it, and return. Naturally, strategy considerations would demand that the turn be made as close to the island as possible.

When the ship piloted by Menoetes drew near to the island, he decided to "play it safe" and swing widely around the rocks. The ship's commander, Gyas, furiously swore at Menoetes to hove closer to the island; when Menoetes refused, Gyas grabbed him and pitched him overboard. The old sea captain struggled to swim to shore, barely making it; he was a pitiable sight as he dragged himself up onto the rocks, dripping wet and spitting out salt water. Observers on the ships enjoyed a hearty laugh at the poor man's expense (Vergil *Aeneid* 5.124–285).

Ball Games

Various kinds of throwing, catching, and bouncing ball games were popular with the Romans, perhaps none more so than *trigon*, a game the *Oxford Classical Dictionary* says was "played by three players standing to form a triangle." It was apparently similar to three-sided catch, in which the players threw the ball (*trigonalis*) to one another. Points could evidently be earned or lost with catches or drops, respectively. Martial's (ca. A.D. 40–ca. 104) Menogenes used to hang around well-to-do *trigon* players and shag missed throws for them, hoping thereby to wangle a dinner invitation (*Epigrams* 12.82).

A certain amount of agility was required to play the game well. The anonymous author of the *Panegyric on Piso* (first century A.D.) refers to Piso's ability to "lay out" (i.e., to make diving catches, thus keeping the ball in play) and somehow to throw the ball to the next player, all in the same motion. So great was Piso's skill that other players would halt their own games to watch him work his ball-playing magic.

Martial indicates in several places (e.g., *Epigrams* 14.49) that ambidextrousness was highly advantageous for a *trigon* player. And a certain Lucius Caecilius once complained when given only 50,000 sesterces for playing *trigon* with the emperor Caligula when the other players received 100,000: "What's the meaning of this? Did I only use one hand?" (Macrobius *Saturnalia* 2.6).

Trigon seemed to be the most physically demanding of the ball games. For example, games played with the *follis* (a large, inflated ball) were better suited for young boys and old men (Martial *Epigrams* 14.47).

Board Games

Ludus Latrunculorum, or Latrunculi. Literally "Robbers," this game was apparently similar to chess because the capture of an opponent's game pieces played a major role in determining the outcome. Some of the pieces were as follows: (1) *latro* ("robber," often with the adjective *vitreus*, "glassy"); (2) *bellator* ("fighter" or "warrior"); (3) *miles* ("soldier"; the term may be interchangeable with *bellator*); (4) *mandra* ("cattle train"). The generic term for "game piece" was *calculus*.

The game was played on a board called the *tabula lusoria*, "gaming board" or "counting board." Some *tabulae lusoriae* could be quite ornate; Petronius (first century A.D.) describes the one owned by Trimalchio as constructed of terebinth wood (a very expensive material), with game pieces made of crystal (*Satyricon* 33.2).

Martial (*Epigrams* 7.72) writes of a certain Paulus, apparently adept at the game, and briefly recounts Paulus's strategy against two opponents, Novius and Publius: to win by closing them in with his *mandrae* ("cattle trains") and his *vitreus latro* ("glassy robber"). Would this indicate that a player had multiple *mandrae* (like pawns in chess) but only one *latro* (like the king or queen)? Ovid (43 B.C.–A.D. 17) also refers to the capture of one piece by multiples of another: *unus cum gemino calculus hoste perit,* "one piece dies when [trapped by] a double enemy." Ovid also indicates a hierarchy, when he suggests that a *miles* may be captured by a *vitreo hoste* ("glass enemy"), an apparent reference to a *latro* (Ovid *Art of Love* 2.208; 3.358).

Some players took the game very seriously. A certain Julius Canus, having run afoul of the emperor Caligula (ruled A.D. 37–41), was imprisoned and ordered to be executed. But in the ten days between his sentencing and his death, he showed no anxiety; in fact, he spent much of that time playing Latrunculi. He was in the midst of a game on the very day on which he was delivered over for the final blow. Before leaving the gaming table, however, he counted up his *calculi* and found that he was one piece ahead of his opponent. "See to it that you don't lie that you won, after I'm dead!" he admonished him. And then, turning to the jailer, he said: "You'll be my witness that I was ahead by one!" (Seneca *On Tranquility of Mind* 14).

The most complete description of moves and tactics in the game comes from the pen of the unknown first century A.D. author of the *Panegyric on Piso*:

[I]n more cunning fashion a piece is moved into different positions and the contest is waged to a finish with glass soldiers (*milites vitrei*), so that white checks the black pieces, and black checks white [reminiscent of chess]. But what player has not retreated before you? What piece is lost when you are its player? Or what piece before capture has not reduced the enemy? In a thousand ways your army fights: one piece, as it retreats, itself captures its pursuer: a reserve piece, standing on the alert, comes from its distant retreat—this one dares to join the fray and cheats the enemy coming for his spoil. Another piece submits to risky delays and, seemingly checked, itself checks two more: this one moves toward higher results, so that, quickly played and breaking the opponent's defensive line, it may burst out on his forces and, when the rampart is down, devastate the enclosed city.... You win with your phalanx intact or deprived of only a few men, and both your hands rattle with the crowd of pieces you have taken. (*Panegyric on Piso* 192–208; trs. J. Wight Duff, Arnold M. Duff LCL)

Duodecim Scripta. Literally "Twelve Lines," this game was apparently similar to backgammon. J.P.V.D. Balsdon provides an excellent description:

Duodecim scripta was played on a board marked out in twenty-four squares, marked successively one to twelve in the first row and then backwards from thirteen to twenty-four in the second, square 24 being directly above square 1. ... Each player had fifteen pieces, and moves were determined by the throwing of three dice. At the start of the game the white pieces were on square 1 and moved forward, the black on square 24, moving backwards. The winner was the player who first succeeded in moving all his pieces from square 1 to square 24, or from square 24 to square 1. . . . If one enemy piece was on the square to which your throw took you, it was driven back to base; if two or more enemy pieces held the square, then you yourself could not occupy it. (Balsdon, *Life and Leisure in Ancient Rome* 156)

Twelve Lines, like Robbers, relied on strategy more than luck. Quintilian (ca. A.D. 35–ca. 90) relates the story of (Publius Mucius?) Scaevola, who, after having been defeated in a game of Twelve Lines, kept mentally reviewing every move he had made; this pensive second-guessing continued even as Scaevola was traveling from Rome into the countryside. Finally, after determining which move had cost him the game, he returned to Rome, located his victorious opponent, and asked him if his analysis had been correct. The other man confirmed Scaevola's suspicions (Quintilian *Institutes of Oratory* 11.2).

Dicing and Gambling   Many Romans were inveterate dice players; although gambling was illegal, the games of chance went on. *Aleam ludere,* "to play at dice" or "to gamble," was a favorite pastime even of some emperors.

Roman dice came in two sizes: large dice—*tali*—marked on four sides with the numbers one, three, four, and six; and small dice—*tesserae*—inscribed on all six sides with numbers one through six. Games with *tesserae* were generally played for higher stakes, and most games required the use of three or four dice.

Certain number combinations, then as now, were more desirable than others. The dog (*canis*) was among the worst: apparently, all one's. Ovid and Propertius both refer to "dog" throws as *damnosi,* "ruinous"; the word *damnosi* implies that a financial loss was inevitable with a "dog" throw (Ovid *Art of Love* 2.206; Propertius *Elegies* 4.8.46).

The best throw? "Venus," whereby all different numbers turned up. Propertius (*Elegies* 4.8.45) attached the adjective *secunda,* "lucky," to the "Venus" throw.

In three different letters (two to Tiberius, and one to his daughter), Augustus (ruled 27 B.C.–A.D. 14) described his dicing and gambling habits (Suetonius *Life of Augustus* 71; tr. John Rolfe LCL)

I dined, dear Tiberius, with the same company. . . . We gambled like old men during the meal both yesterday and today; for when the dice were thrown, whoever turned up the "dog" or the six, put a denarius in the pool for each one of the dice, and the whole was taken by anyone who threw the "Venus."

We spent the Quinquatria [the March festival of Minerva] very merrily, my dear Tiberius, for we played all day long and kept the gaming-board warm. Your brother made a great outcry about his luck, but after all did not come out far behind in the long run; for after losing heavily, he unexpectedly and little by little got back a good deal. For my part, I lost twenty thousand sesterces, but because I was extravagantly generous in my play, as usual. If I had demanded of everyone the stakes which I let go, or had kept all that I gave away, I should have won fully fifty thousand. But I like that better, for my generosity will exalt me to immortal glory.

I send you two hundred and fifty denarii, the sum which I gave each of my guests, in case they wished to play at dice or at odd and even during the dinner.

Leisure Activities of Two Roman Notables

Marcus Aurelius as an Athlete. Although the emperor Marcus Aurelius (ruled A.D. 161–180) was best known for his administrative skills and his philosophical musings, he also enjoyed various athletic pursuits, including boxing, wrestling, racing, hunting, and especially ball playing, at which he attained a great deal of proficiency (Scriptores Historiae Augustae *Life of Marcus Aurelius* 4).

Seneca as a Nonathlete. Seneca (4 B.C.–A.D. 65) notes that most successful athletes have to train rigorously if they want to succeed. They undergo all manner of physical pain to prepare themselves: *exercitatio ipsa tormentum est*, "the training itself is torture."

Seneca himself did not much care for competitive athletics, at least if he had to participate. He describes his two leisure-time activities after reaching the golden years: *stratum* and *lectio*, "bed" and "books," that is, resting and reading. He does not need to devote much time to exercise because as soon as he starts he gets tired, a condition that he claims is the end result for even the most physically fit.

His *progymnastes*, "personal trainer," was a very young slave boy named Pharius, who once remarked that he and Seneca must have been the same age, because both were losing their teeth! Whenever the two went jogging, it took almost no time before a huge gap opened up between trainer and master (Seneca *Moral Epistles* 78; 83).

REFERENCES

Ausonius: *Epistles*.
Balsdon, J.P.V.D.: *Life and Leisure in Ancient Rome*.
Cato the Elder: *On Agriculture*.
Cicero: *Letters to Atticus; Letters to His Brother Quintus; Philippics*.
Dionysius of Halicarnassus: *Roman Antiquities*.
Horace: *Odes; Satires*.
Livy: *From the Founding of the City*.
Macrobius: *Saturnalia*.
Martial: *Epigrams*.
Ovid: *Art of Love; Tristia*.
Panegyric on Piso (author unknown).
Petronius: *Satyricon*.
Plautus: *Pot of Gold*.

Pliny the Younger: *Natural History*.
Plutarch: *Life of Camillus*.
Propertius: *Elegies*.
Quintilian: *Institutes of Oratory*.
Scriptores Historiae Augustae: *Life of Marcus Aurelius*.
Seneca: *Moral Epistles; On Tranquility of Mind*.
Statius: *Forests*.
Suetonius: *Life of Augustus; Life of Julius Caesar; Life of Nero*.
Tacitus: *Annals*.
Vergil: *Aeneid*.

9

Sports and Amusements

AT THE RACETRACK

A crisp autumn afternoon in A.D. 146. Although a slight chill permeates the air, it does not deter the 250,000 fans from the Circus Maximus, Rome's colossal chariot racetrack. They settle into their seats to watch the great driver of the Red team, Appuleius Diocles, compete in what may be the final race of his storied career.

An Outstanding Charioteer: Appuleius Diocles

The twelve drivers and their rigs position themselves in the starting gates. Suddenly the signal is given, and the twelve thunder forth. One lap, two, three are completed; with four to go, Diocles has managed to maintain his early lead and even extend it. Dust and sand, thrown into the air by 192 pounding hooves, create a hazy scene on the track.

The drivers and their horses made the circuit a fourth time, then a fifth and sixth. The deafening roar of the crowd continues on its crescendo as the final lap approaches. Many of the 250,000, having placed hefty wagers on Diocles, do not contain their excitement as they see him in the forefront of the pack.

Now to the backstretch, then home. Diocles, Rome's premier charioteer, hangs on to the lead, claiming yet another victory. The adoring multitude showers him with praise and cheering as he moves slowly from the track to the dressing room.

Appuleius Diocles shone forth as one of the near deities in the Roman chariot racing pantheon. His career spanned twenty-four years; from the time he began competing professionally—at age 18 in A.D. 122—until the day he retired, he won 1,462 races.

And he won them in every imaginable way: with two-horse teams and four-horse teams—and once even with seven horses. He won them by taking the lead at the start and maintaining it throughout. He won them by deliberately falling behind at the outset and then relying on a surge at the end. He won them without using a whip or by plying the whip, as needed. He won high-stakes races and races offering minimal payouts. He won as a member of the weakest team of racers, the White faction, and he won as a member of the more powerful teams, the Red, Blue, and Green factions. He won singles races in which every charioteer competed for himself; he won team races in which members of the same faction cooperated tactically to ensure victory for one of their teammates. He won his first race in 124 at the age of 20; he was still winning races as a fortysomething graybeard.

A lengthy inscription—probably carved to commemorate his retirement from racing—provides many interesting details about his career (*CIL* 6.10048). In particular, his 1,462 victories are itemized according to the various tactics that he most often successfully used:

Latin Term	Probable English Translation	Number of Victories Using This Tactic
Occupavit et vicit	He won by holding the lead throughout	815
Successit et vicit	He won by coming from behind	67
Praemisit et vicit	He won by deliberately falling behind at the outset	36
Variis generibus vicit	He won in miscellaneous ways	42
Eripuit et vicit	He won on the homestretch	502
		1,462 total victories

The last entry, *eripuit et vicit*, seems not to describe a tactic but rather a situation; and the meaning of this phrase has been much debated. However, the use of the verb *eripuit* ("to snatch away," often quickly or unexpectedly) seems to indicate a race whose outcome was in doubt until the final seconds. In any event, the phrase receives additional itemization in the inscription. Diocles "snatched away" victory from the Green Faction 216 times, from the Blue on 205 occasions, and from the White 81 times (total: 502).

And during the course of all this occupying, seizing, snatching, and holding, Appuleius Diocles became wealthy, amassing over 35,000,000 sesterces in prize money over the course of his long career. (By contrast, the average laborer or craftsman in Diocles' day could expect to earn perhaps 60,000 sesterces per year, or roughly 1,440,000 in twenty-four years.) By the time his career ended, he had earned enough money to purchase a home in the fashionable retirement community of Praeneste.

The inscriptional account of Diocles' life and career is so detailed that we could construct from it an end-of-career résumé that might look something like this:

Name: Appuleius Diocles

Date of birth: A.D. 104

Place of birth: Lusitania (Spain)

Career objective: professional charioteer

Career outline:

—A.D. 122: began racing chariots (age 18), with the White Faction

—A.D. 124: won my first race

—A.D. 128: joined Green Faction; briefly with Blue Faction

—A.D. 131: joined Red Faction; stayed with Reds for the remainder of my career

—A.D. 146: retired after twenty-four years as a charioteer

Accomplishments:

—4,257 races, with 1,462 wins

—career winning percentage: .343

—2,900 first, second, or third place finishes

—my 134 wins in A.D. 131 set a record for most wins by a charioteer in one season of racing

—the eight 50,000-sesterces prizes that I won set a record

—I was the first to race with a seven-horse team

—prize money won: 35,860,120 sesterces

By the end of the first century A.D., chariot racetracks had appeared all over the Roman world, from Spain in the west to the Levant in the east to Africa in the south. But the grandest and gaudiest track of all was located in Rome itself; **Racetrack Facilities** it was named—without an iota of understatement—the Circus Maximus, "Greatest Racetrack."

The Circus Maximus, supposedly designed and built sometime during the monarchy (753–509 B.C.), underwent several renovations over the course of the following centuries. By Diocles' time it could accommodate 250,000 racing fans. And they were rabid fans. Their roars and cheers could be heard for miles; the poet Juvenal informs us that when passing by the Circus, he could tell merely by the crowd noise which faction had won a race.

It was long enough to contain six football fields. The central dividing wall (*spina*), around which the chariots completed their seven laps, was decorated with obelisks and other trophies captured by the far-flung Roman armies. The twelve starting gates, sited at the far end of the structure, were laid out not in a straight line but on the arc of a circle, to ensure a fair start for all twelve of their occupants.

Organization of Roman Chariot Racing
Professional charioteers in the city of Rome were organized into first two, and later four, teams called factions. These factions were colorfully named:

Latin Team Name	English Translation
Factio Alba	White Faction
Factio Russata	Red Faction
Factio Veneta	Blue Faction
Factio Prasina	Green Faction

It appears that the White Faction was the weakest of the four and that many drivers, including Diocles, began their careers as members of the Whites. If these rookie drivers showed some promise and could notch some victories while wearing the white, they might advance to one of the stronger factions. It is clear that charioteers could and did move from one faction to another; Diocles, of course, raced for all four factions at one time or another during his long stint on the track. What is not clear is the system that regulated the charioteers' mobility. Did they get traded from one faction to another? Could they at some point become free agents, signing with the faction that offered the most money, in the manner of modern professional athletes? Could they be released by one faction and catch on with another? These are some of the tantalizingly unanswerable questions about Roman chariot racing.

A Day at the Races
On the major racing days, there may have been as many as twelve or even sixteen races. The first race of the day was generally preceded by a ceremonial lap (*pompa*) around the *spina*; to win the first race of the day, immediately after the *pompa*, was deemed a particular distinction.

The race began when the presiding magistrate dropped a white napkin (*mappa*); this served as the starting signal.

The drivers were required to complete seven laps around the *spina*. And what action-packed laps they were! Few if any rules governed the tactics employed Diocles and his colleagues. Blocking a rival, forcing or causing collisions, and/or making swift and unexpected lane changes were all permissible. Charioteers increased their risk of injury by their habit of looping or tying the slack of the reins around their waists; even though such a practice undoubtedly provided a driver with better leverage in controlling his horses, it could also spell doom should the unfortunate rein-entangled man be ejected from the chariot, for then he would almost certainly be dragged along on the ground by his out-of-control horses. So although the best charioteers could become fabulously wealthy, charioteering was certainly not a profession for the faint of heart!

On rare occasions a race might end in a dead heat, "too close to call." In that event, the two contestants raced an eighth lap to determine the winner.

Although Diocles was certainly one of ancient Rome's best known prime-time charioteers, he was not the only one. Consider, for example, the accomplishments of Publius Aelius Gutta Calpurnianus, winner of 1,127 races. Calpurnianus, like Diocles, raced for all four factions; an **Other Noteworthy Charioteers** inscription (*CIL* 6.10047) detailing Calpurnianus's career indicates that he won 583 times for the Blues, 364 for the Greens, 78 for the Reds, and 102 for the Whites.

An odd Latin phrase appearing in the Calpurnianus inscription is *pedibus ad quadrigam*, "on foot toward the chariot," a technique he used in sixty-one of his Green Faction wins. But how could such a strategy be executed in the throes of a hotly contested chariot race? Some think that the phrase refers to races in which the charioteers dismounted at some point and finished the race on foot.

Imagine the improbable scene: some drivers reaching the dismount point ahead of others and then trying to avoid being trampled to death by drivers still in their chariots! Besides, Latin vocabulary cries out against this interpretation; the preposition *ad* means "to" or "toward," not "out of."

More likely, *pedibus ad quadrigam* describes the start of the race, when charioteers ran from some unspecified point on the track toward their waiting chariots. But in any case, we can presume that the footrace/chariot race hybrid was short-lived, because the term appears nowhere but in the Calpurnianus inscription.

The inscription concludes with a noteworthy boast: *Hoc monumentum vivus feci*, "I constructed this monument while still alive." Serious injury and death were a charioteer's constant companions, and any who could compete over long periods and live to tell their tales deserved special mention.

One of the most successful charioteers of all—if the ancient sources are accurate—was the first century A.D. driver Flavius Scorpus, who tallied an astounding 2,048 victories. Charioteers did not often grace the pages of litterateurs, but Martial made an exception in the case of Scorpus; the poet mentions him in six epigrams. From these we learn that Scorpus was not yet 30 years of age when he died (presumably as a result of a racing accident); that he was (like Diocles) extremely wealthy, a charioteer whose prowess enabled him to earn fifteen heavy bags of gold in only one hour of racing; that his skills were so widely known that spectators frequently placed bets on him.

Other celebrated charioteers:

- Marcus Aurelius Mollicius Tatianus, who won 125 races, even though he died before his twenty-first birthday.
- Marcus Aurelius Polynices, who triumphed 739 times, including 655 during his tenure with the Red Faction. Polynices was apparently something of an innovator as well: he won eight races with an eight-horse rig, nine with a ten-horse rig, and three with a seven-horse rig.
- Lacerta (full name possibly Gaius Annius Lacerta), a Red Faction driver whom the poet/satirist Juvenal (*Satires* 7.112–114) offered as an example of the tremendous wealth that successful charioteers could amass. In Lacerta's case, that wealth amounted to 100 times the net worth of a well-to-do lawyer.
- Musclosus, another highly successful Red Faction driver. Of his 682 career victories, 672 came while he wore the Red. He also won three times for the Whites, five for the Greens, and two for the Blues (*CIL* 6.10063).

Not all charioteers enjoyed success on a Dioclean, Calpurnianan, or Scorpan scale, however. The charioteer Scirtus raced for thirteen years, from A.D. 13 to 25, and won only eleven times in that period. His career was noteworthy in that he spent all thirteen years in the White Faction, an indication, perhaps, that the managers of the other factions did not see in him much potential for success.

The inscription (*CIL* 6.10051) that preserves the details of Scirtus's career lists the number of races that he won in each of his thirteen years, as well as the number of second and third place finishes:

Year	Firsts*	Seconds	Thirds
A.D. 13	1	1	1
14	1	1	2
15	1	2	5
16	3	5	5
17	3	8	6
18	0	7	12
19	1	5	5
20	0	3	4
21	0	2	5
22	0	3	4
23	1	1	5
24	0	1	4
25	0	0	2

Note: *Includes races designated *revocatus*, those won (apparently) on a re-run, when the initial finish was too close to call.

Scirtus's career displays a quasi bell-shaped curve, characteristic of many professional athletes throughout history: limited success in the early years, followed by an increase in proficiency in the "prime time" years, followed by an end-of-career decline.

Most charioteers probably accepted the possibility of severe injury as one of the inevitable drawbacks of the profession. **Injuries** Fortunately, remedies and cures were available. Pliny the Elder (*Natural History* 28.237–238) recommends applying boar dung on bruises or pulled muscles that a charioteer might incur after being dragged behind his chariot or run over by another. He also reports that boar dung could be added in powdered form to vinegar or wine and taken internally. This concoction allegedly hastened the healing of muscle pulls and strains.

Of course, charioteers would have gone nowhere, would have won nothing, if not for the other prime factor in the sport: the **Horses** horses. Pliny the Elder provides some of the basics about the animals, stating that military horses had physiques not suited for the racetrack and that the optimum age for a racing horse was 5 years.

Pliny also had a healthy respect for the intelligence and race sense of Circus horses, as he relates in the following story:

Horses harnessed to chariots in the circus unquestionably show that they understand the shouts of encouragement and applause. At the races in the circus forming part of the Secular Games of Claudius Caesar, a charioteer of the Whites named Raven was thrown at the start, and his team took the lead and kept it by getting in the way of their rivals and jostling them aside and doing everything against them that they would have to do with a most skillful charioteer in control, and as they were ashamed for human science to be beaten by horses, when they had completed the proper course [they came to a dead stop at the finish line]. (Pliny the Elder *Natural History* 28.159; tr. LCL H. Rackham)

Two long inscriptions survive that are devoted entirely to listing the names of race horses. The first of these (*CIL* 6.10053) records 74 names, the second (*CIL* 6.10056) 122 names.

These equine names fall into several categories, including mythological figures: Polynices, Phaedrus, Ajax, Arion, Daedalus and Argo (but, oddly, none was named after famous mythological horses such as Pegasus or Bellerophon). Descriptive names appear: Virilis (Strong), Superbus (Confident), Hilarus (Cheery), Cirratus (Curly), Barbatus (Bearded), Callinicus (Beautiful Winner), Frugifer (Profitable), Eminens (Outstanding), Praesidium (Fortress), Reburrus (Bristling).

Some horses bore various animal names: Aranius (Spider), Acceptor (Hawk), Perdix (Partridge), Murinus (Mousey), Aquila (Eagle), Lupus (Wolf), Leo (Lion), Bubalus (Gazelle), Passerinus (Little Sparrow)—

whereas others had geographical names: Aegyptus (Egypt), Lybius (Lybian), Maurus (Moorish), Indus (Indian), Tyrrhenus (Tyrrhenian). And then there were sinister or threatening names: Raptor (Thief), Latro (Bandit), Vastator (Destroyer), Rapax (Plundering), Pugio (Dagger), Ballista (Missile), Sagitta (Arrow).

The number of victories credited to each horse is also recorded. Some noteworthy totals: Olympus, 152; Faustus, 128; Indus, 116; Leo, 58. The vast majority of the 196 horses, however, won fewer than a half-dozen races, and only a handful even reached double-digit victory totals.

IN THE AMPHITHEATER

A Famous Gladiator: Celadus "the Heartthrob"
Mid-afternoon on a hot summer day in Pompeii. The local amphitheater is filled with some 10,000 gladiatorial aficionados, all of them tensed and ready for the long-awaited appearance of Celadus, one of the most famed gladiators of the day. Many in the crowd are women; Celadus's widely known nickname, Suspirium Puellarum ("Heartthrob of the Girls") had not been bestowed upon him without good reason.

Finally, the big moment arrives. Celadus strides forth from the bowels of the amphitheater into the light of day. His burnished armor gleams; the crest on his helmet waves gently in the breeze. The crowd rises to its feet, the noise of their screaming and cheering rocking the foundations of the venerable structure that has been the site of so many matches over the years. Celadus turns to face his opponent. The match begins . . .

Modern moralists decry and denigrate the Romans for tolerating and even promoting the inhumane brutality of gladiatorial combat. One noted commentator, Michael Grant, in *Roman Gladiators*, claimed that "the two most quantitatively destructive institutions in history are Nazism and the Roman gladiators." But a sober and balanced study of the subject reveals that such combats were not necessarily the bloodbaths they are often reputed to have been, nor were gladiators merciless killing machines bent on murder and mayhem. The Romans were not even the first civilization to engage in such activities. Stories of nonmilitary one-on-one armed combat can be found in Homer's *Iliad*. The Celts and the Etruscans were known to have enjoyed such spectacles. Clearly, gladiatorial shows were not invented by the Romans.

Types of Gladiators
The ranks of gladiators were filled from several sources, including, oddly enough, freeborn Roman citizens who might either be drafted for service or volunteer.

Asinius Pollio (76 B.C.–A.D. 5) describes in a letter to Cicero the shocking circumstances surrounding the compulsory gladiatorial service of Fadius, a Roman soldier serving under Pompey:

At the gladiatorial shows, there was a certain Fadius, a soldier of Pompey; he had been pressed into the gladiatorial school, and having twice defeated his adversary without being paid for it, he objected to binding himself over to be a gladiator, and had sought refuge among the people. So [Lucius Cornelius] Balbus [a Roman quaestor] first let loose some Gallic horsemen among the crowd—for stones were thrown at him when Fadius was being dragged away—and then carried off Fadius, buried him up to the waist in the gladiator's school, and burned him alive, while he [Balbus], having lunched, strolled about bare-footed with his tunic ungirdled and his hands behind his back, and when the poor wretch shrieked out, "I am born a Roman citizen" [and hence not subject to capital punishment without due process], he answered, "Off with you at once; implore the protection of the people." (Cicero *Letters to His Friends* 10.32; tr. W. Glynn Williams LCL)

Gladiators were grouped in about sixteen different categories or classifications, depending on the type of armor and costuming they wore. Of these, the most readily identifiable were the Thraeces (Thracians); *murmillones; retiarii* ("netmen"); *secutores* ("pursuers"); and *essedarii* ("chariot fighters").

Thraeces. The dress and armament of Thracian gladiators are best illustrated by artistic representations. A series of stucco reliefs from the tomb of Scaurus at Pompeii shows activities of various types of gladiators; several of these have been identified as Thracians. It is clear that the Thracians wore visored helmets; had full-length arm bands, at least on the right arm; carried a small shield, either round or square; had protective coverings on the legs from waist to knee; and were equipped with (sometimes) elaborate knee-to-foot shin guards. They also brandished a short, curved sword called a *sica*.

Murmillones. The *murmillones* are mentioned fairly often in Roman literature and inscriptions, but little information is forthcoming about their dress and equipment. They were probably helmeted, and they may have carried a sword or a club; on the whole, however, it appears that they were lightly armed, without an abundance of protective armor.

Retiarii. The "netmen" are the most fully documented of all classes of gladiators, and also the most uniquely equipped. They were the only gladiators who fought without any protection for the head. They wore a short tunic of some sort, as well as leggings, a wide cummerbund, and a sleeve on the left arm, to which was appended a leather or metal shoulder pad to take the place of a shield. The shoulder padding was evidently fairly prominent, so much so that it was referred to by the word *galerus*, "helmet," a sort of helmet for the shoulder.

The *retiarii* carried several offensive weapons, one of which, the net, gave rise to their title, "netmen." Skillful wielding of the net was crucial; failure to entangle the arms or legs of their opponents could have disastrous, or at least embarrassing, consequences for the *retiarii*. These gladiators also carried a trident and a dagger. They attempted to win their matches by using their metal weapons in consort with the net.

Secutores. A secutor ("pursuer") was often matched against a *retiarius*, for obvious reasons. The lumbering *secutor* was heavily armed and armored, with a large crested helmet; chest, shoulder, and leg protection; and a sword and shield. Thus weighed down, he must have found it frustrating sometimes to have to chase the lightly equipped, usually agile *retiarius* around the arena floor.

Essedarii. The *essedarii* were perhaps the most bizarre of all gladiatorial classes: gladiators who fought from chariots. This phenomenon apparently had British origins; when Julius Caesar visited the island in the 50's B.C., he provided this description:

Their manner of fighting from chariots is as follows. First of all they drive in all directions and hurl missiles, and so by the mere terror that the teams inspire and by the noise of the wheels they generally throw ranks into confusion. When they have worked their way in between the troops of cavalry, they leap down from the chariots and fight on foot. Meanwhile the charioteers retire gradually from the combat, and dispose the chariots in such fashion that, if the warriors are hard pressed by the host of the enemy, they may have a ready means of retirement to their own side. Thus they show in action the mobility of cavalry and the stability of infantry; and by daily use and practice they become so accomplished that they are ready to gallop their teams down the steepest of slopes without loss of control, to check and turn them in a moment, to run along the pole, stand on the yoke, and then, quick as lightning, to dart back into the chariot. (Julius Caesar *Gallic Wars* 4.33; tr. H. J. Edwards LCL)

Individual Gladiators Much of our information about individual gladiators comes from tombstones; the inscriptions are generally short and formulaic, containing some or all of the following: the gladiator's name, his age at death, his classification, his birthplace, the name of the person who paid for his tombstone, and perhaps a few scraps of information about his career. Some examples:

- The *murmillo* Columbus Serenianus, an Aeduan, fought twenty-five matches; his wife, Sperata, set up his monument (*CIL* 5.3325).

- The Thracian Apollonius fought six matches. It is also recorded on his tombstone that he was a left-handed gladiator, apparently an oddity. But southpaws would have had something of an advantage: the artistic representations of armed gladiators often depict them wearing protective coverings on the left side of the body only, with corresponding right-side portions of their anatomy unprotected. Right-handed sword-wielding opponents would thus have struck padding, but lefties would have had a clear shot at exposed skin (*CIL* 6.10196).

- Marcus Ulpius Felix, a Gallic *murmillo*, lived to the age of 45; when he died his wife, Ulpia Syntyche, and his son, Justus, placed his monument (*CIL* 6.10177).

• The Syrian secutor Flamma, who lived to the age of 30, fought 34 matches; he won 21 of these and fought to a no-decision in the other 13 (*CIL* 10.7297).

Names of gladiators seldom found their way into the writings of respectable Roman authors, but exceptions do exist. Lucilius, Horace, and Cicero all mention the second (?) century B.C. gladiator Pacideianus, often considered one of the best in the business. The violence and ferocity with which he fought are illustrated by his unique method of "psyching himself up" before a match: "I'll first take his blow in my face; then I'll stick my sword into the fool's stomach and lungs. I hate the idiot! I'm out of control when I fight!"

The reference to taking a hit in the face seems to be a reflection of a part of the unwritten gladiatorial code: namely, that gladiators preferred to absorb blows rather than to avoid them, for avoiding blows was apparently considered cowardly.

In the gladiatorial context, paired chariots, manned by two *essedarii* apiece (a driver and a gladiator), evidently drove to some central location in the arena, where the fighters dismounted and battled on foot.

Gladiatorial shows took place in amphitheaters, oval structures found in numerous cities throughout the Roman world. The most well known of these amphitheaters was undoubtedly the Coliseum in Rome.

Amphitheater Facilities

Construction on this architectural wonder in ancient Rome began in A.D. 80; in the following year the building was dedicated with a magnificent opening-day celebration. The Coliseum (known as the Flavian Amphitheater in Roman times) was clearly built to colossal standards: nearly 400 feet long, with 180-foot-high outer walls, it could accommodate about 50,000 spectators. Its 80 arched entrances, 23 feet high and all numbered, allowed for easy entrance and exiting.

Another amazing feature: the arena floor could be flooded with water, for the mock naval battles that were occasionally presented there.

In order to ensure that the Coliseum and other amphitheaters would be filled with spectators on "game day," gladiatorial shows were advertised in advance, usually via announcements painted on public walls and buildings. These posters generally contained the following information: date(s) and sponsor(s) of shows; number of gladiators scheduled to perform; names of well-known gladiators who would appear; descriptions of promotional gimmicks (e.g., door prizes) or special amenities (e.g., canvas awnings to shade the seating areas).

Two millennia later, what are we to make of an Appuleius Diocles, a Celadus, a Calpurnianus, or a Pacideianus? Were they brutal and inhumane egotists, bent on personal advancement regardless of the cost to others? Would we agree with Juvenal's bitter complaint that the Roman people would be content as long as they had full bellies and live entertainment? ("Bread and circuses" was his famous way of wording it.) Can we not view these gifted athletes—for that is surely what they were—as human beings not all that different from their counterparts in any other era of history: men who had wives and children and the obligation to support them, while at the same time providing a few hours of excitement on a hot summer afternoon for tens of thousands of their fellow Romans. Even a grouch like Juvenal would certainly have seen some value in that!

LOWLIFE CHARACTERS

Like any world superpower, the ancient Romans were plagued by low-lifes and scofflaws, boors and bores, thieves and vandals. Their names and deeds abounded in the pages of writers like Catullus, Pliny the Younger, and Martial; their doings were etched into graffiti-covered walls in Rome and Pompeii. In their own immoral way, they achieved a little piece of immortality, no less enduring than that of a Caesar or a Cicero.

Legacy Hunters   Martial told the tales of a number of men who sought the hands of old dowagers in marriage; these legacy hunters were known as *captators*. Gemellus, for example, wanted to marry Maronilla, the ugliest woman around. Her attraction? She had a bad cough.

And then there was a certain Calenus, whose net worth of 2,000,000 sesterces increased to 10,000,000 over the course of only seven months. What could have accounted for this sudden upturn? Four deaths (Martial *Epigrams* 1.94).

Poor Bithynicus fell victim to a little table-turning in the legacy hunting game. He courted the aged Naevia, a wheezing, sneezing, coughing, spitting old lady—who was faking the symptoms to gain his attentions (2.26).

Saleianus, usually a happy man, wore an expression of gloom one day when Martial chanced to meet up with him. Saleianus's wife had died—Secundilla, that old Secundilla, that rich Secundilla, who increased Saleianus's net worth by a cool one million sesterces. Martial expressed his sincere regrets to his friend, whose face bore the track of many a crocodile tear (2.65).

Is the phrase "greedy *captator*" redundant? Martial briefly tells the story of Africanus, a millionaire who continued to dig for dowager gold: *Fortuna multis dat nimis, satis nulli*, "Luck gives way too much to lots of people, but enough to no one" (12.10).

Martial does not specifically identify Polycharmus as a legacy hunter, but he does say this: Polycharmus was sickly, often lying abed ten times a year, or more, with various ailments. Every time he "recovered," he was showered with gifts from his relieved friends. "Polycharmus, get sick once and for all" was Martial's wry comment (12.56).

Clytus used a somewhat related ploy to extract presents from friends: he claimed to have eight birthdays a year. It seemed as if virtually every first of every month was Clytus's birthday. His face was smooth, his hair jet black, no signs whatsoever of advanced age, and yet he was apparently older than even a Priam or a Nestor, two of Greek mythology's grand old men. Martial warns Clytus not to overdo the "birthday thing," or soon his friends will consider him not to have been born at all—hence no more presents, not even on his one true birthday (8.64).

For the sad story of a legacy hunt that backfired, we could turn yet again to Martial and his description of the *captator* Labienus. A certain Fabius left Labienus his entire estate, but it turned out to be hardly worth Labienus's trouble: his gift-giving to the old man had outvalued the entirety of the inheritance he received (7.66).

A similarly disappointed *captator* was Bithynicus. He gave old Fabius (maybe the same one as above) 6,000 sesterces per year. But when Fabius died and the will was read, not a sesterce was bequeathed to Bithynicus. Martial urged Bithynicus to look on the bright side: at least each year, he could save the 6,000 (9.9).

Martial also introduces us to Marianus, an old (naturally!), wealthy (naturally!) gentleman pursued by an unnamed legacy hunter in the same way that a fisherman pursues a fish: he baits the hook with costly gifts, hoping to be named in Marianus's will. But Martial asks whether the fisherman will grieve when Marianus dies. The only way for Marianus to ensure that his pursuer weeps tears of true sorrow: cut him out of the will (6.63).

More fishing imagery: Martial claims that Gargilianus sent *munera ingentia*, "colossal presents," to old codgers and aged dowagers alike. Presents, did he say? Much more like the bait that fishermen and hunters used to snare unwary fish or beasts. If Gargilianus should ever have wished to discover the difference between gifts and bribes, he had only to send some of those mountains of sesterces Martial's way (4.55).

In a move reminiscent of modern-day bumper sticker wisdom— "We're spending our children's inheritance"—Crispus made certain that his wife (later widow) would not fall prey to legacy hunters: while still alive, he spent his entire estate on himself (5.32).

Martial himself was not above a little legacy hunting, though perhaps he was not as adept at the trade as some others. He tells of Charinus, who revised his will thirty times in one year; with each new revision, Martial sent the old man expensive honey cakes. After thirty such gifts the poet was broke, whereas Charinus was still going strong. Maybe, Martial laments, Charinus's cough was not as bad as it sounded (5.39).

A twist on the *captator* theme: a profligate son who wasted his father's money. Martial immortalizes the spendthrift Philomusus, whose monthly allowance from his father was 2,000 sesterces. But the young man spent 2,000 per day. When Philomusus's father died, he left his entire fortune to his son: small comfort, because it amounted to nothing (3.10).

Another twist on the *captator* theme: the wealthy Domitius Tullus, while alive, egged on the legacy hunters by accepting their gifts and the other benefactions that they willingly bestowed upon him. But when he died and his will was read, it was found that he had left his entire estate to his family. Not so much as a single sestertium was to find its way to the moneybelts of the fortune hunters. The news of the will set off a round of tongue wagging in the city. Some people found the old man guilty of hypocrisy, and worse, for misleading the legacy hunters, whereas others praised his courage and cleverness in turning the tables on men who practiced a disreputable trade (Pliny the Younger *Letters* 8.18).

Gaurus, a wealthy old man, was the recipient of many a gift. The unspoken statement of the givers to Gaurus: "Die. And the sooner the better" (Martial *Epigrams* 8.27).

Pliny the Younger relates the story of one Regulus, who apparently raised the bar of brazen tackiness to new heights. On one occasion a wealthy widow named Verania was facing an imminent demise. Regulus hurried to her bedside and, in the smoothest manner imaginable, asked her for details about the date and time of her birth. Having procured this information, he began mumbling some meaningless mutterings, accompanied by hand gestures of various sorts, finally concluding the show with a promise to Verania that she would fully recover from her ailment. But the ever-benevolent Regulus went one step further: he left the premises to consult certain omens that would (he said!) verify his initial prognostication. Upon his return he proclaimed with the most sincere sounding oaths that his diagnosis was confirmed and that she would soon regain her health. Overjoyed, she rewrote her will on the spot, inserting a provision providing a sizable bequest for the slick-talking Regulus. When shortly thereafter her condition took a turn for the worse, her only anti-Regulan recourse was to scream imprecations at him.

Another intended victim of Regulus: the wealthy and respected Velleius Blaesus. Regulus had heard that Blaesus intended to revise his will; it seemed to Regulus a propitious time to strike up a friendship with the old man. During the affinity-building process, Regulus constantly badgered Blaesus's physicians to do their utmost to keep him alive. But once Regulus's name was entered into the will, his attitude made an about-face; he now begged the medical men to show some mercy to their dying patient and allow him to pass on in peace. The doctors and Blaesus obliged, but the dead man also got the post-mortem last laugh. Suspecting that Regulus was more than a little devoid of sincerity, Blaesus had surreptitiously cancelled his inheritance, leaving Regulus empty-handed.

Would the following be an example of reverse psychology legacy hunting? The *captator* Lupus kept encouraging Urbicus and his wife, Cosconia, to become parents, when actually Lupus was hoping for the opposite to unfold: *ars est captandi quod nolis velle videri*, "The art of the legacy-hunter is to seem to wish what one does not wish" (Pliny the Younger *Letters* 2.20; tr. Walter Ker LCL). If Cosconia ever announced that she were with child, all the color would have drained from Lupus's face. Martial's advice to Urbicus: all questions of fatherhood aside, bequeath nothing to Lupus (*Epigrams* 11.55).

In his essay *On Duties* (3.58–60), Cicero recounts the story of one Gaius Canius, a wealthy and sophisticated Roman gentleman, who once vacationed in Syracuse on the island of Sicily. He made it known that he was interested in buying some property in the area; the information eventually reached the listening ears—and conniving mind—of Pythius, a Syracusan banker. Pythius told Canius that he owned the very sort of beachfront real estate that Canius was seeking, but—sad to say—it was not for sale. However, the money-lender continued, Canius could visit the place if he wished, and Pythius also invited him to join him there the next evening for dinner. Canius agreed.

Scams, Swindles, and Lies

Meanwhile, Pythius rounded up as many fishermen as he could and instructed them to fish en masse outside his estate the next day. Canius arrived for dinner as scheduled and was astonished to look out onto the water to see a veritable armada of fishing boats. One by one, the fishermen brought their catches into the villa. Canius's jaw dropped even more; he asked Pythius to explain the finny phenomenon. The latter claimed that the best fishing spot in all Syracuse was located in the waters off his estate.

Canius begged Pythius to sell, sell, sell. Pythius played it cool, for a while refusing but finally agreeing to "allow" Canius to take the property off his hands—for a very handsome price.

The very next day the exuberant Canius invited a number of his friends to dine at the home overlooking the best fishing hole on the island. But much to his surprise, not a boat was to be seen. Not so much as a net anywhere; and no fish broke the calm surface of the sea with a skyward leap.

Canius hurried to his nextdoor neighbor's house to inquire about the whereabouts of fish and fishermen; were they perhaps taking the day off? The neighbor replied that there was no vacation that day. He went on to say that he was astonished to have seen all the water craft gathered there yesterday, because the fishing in this particular area ranged from awful to horrendous. Only then did Canius realize that he had been scammed. But by then it was too late, and anger was his only recourse.

An Innocent Scam? Aulus Gellius (*Attic Nights* 1.23) preserves the following story, originally told by Cato the Elder.

It seems that at one time in old Rome, senators were permitted to take their young sons with them to senate meetings, which is how the youthful Papirius Praetextatus happened to appear in those chambers from time to time.

The senate had a rule stating that issues not resolved by the close of the working day were to be held in strict confidence by the members and not to be discussed publicly. This very situation arose one day when Papirius was present. Upon his return home, his mother asked him what happened in the senate meeting that day. Young Papirius, aware of the "when-asked-don't-tell" rule, concocted this story: the senate had discussed a pressing social issue, namely, whether it was more advantageous to the state for a husband to have two wives, or a wife two husbands.

The gullible mother, having bought the story hook, line, and wedding band, immediately rushed out to inform her female friends. The next day the women thronged to the senate house, begging the members to endorse a two-man, one-woman arrangement. The senators, naturally, had nary a clue about the reason for this demand for a 2:1 male/female ratio.

At this point young Papirius intervened to explain what he had done. The senate, although impressed by the young man's candor and cleverness, nonetheless noted that from then on, no senator's sons should be allowed to sit in on senate meetings . . . except for Papirius.

A Parallel Story. On another occasion the senate was debating a matter of some importance. Each night, when one of the senators (unfortunately unnamed by Plutarch, teller of the tale) came home, his wife endlessly nagged him to spill the senatorial beans. She promised that she would hold anything he told her in strictest confidence, often concluding her petitions with that ultimate uxorial utterance: "If you really trusted and loved me, you'd tell me!"

One morning the beleaguered husband finally caved in—sort of. He concocted a story that some priests had seen a lark outfitted with a golden helmet and a spear. He said that the senate had been debating for days the significance of this omen. He concluded his fable by reminding his wife to keep a tight lid on her newfound knowledge. This she promised to do. Having extracted the pledge, he left for the forum.

But as soon as the unfortunate man was out of earshot, his wife summoned a serving maid. The astonished maid watched in silence as her mistress cried, screamed, tore at her hair, and beat her chest in an unprecedented display of "oh-woe-is-us." The maid still said nothing; finally, the senator's wife had to order her to ask what was amiss. When the maid complied, the other woman related to her the whole larkish story, ending with the traditionally stern injunction to tell no one. Naturally, however, the maid told a friend, and that friend told a friend, and so on, and so on.

The story spread so fast that it was actually circulating in the forum before the senator arrived there. When he finally did appear, a grim-faced colleague immediately informed him of the sinister omen of the armored lark. The senator laughed and explained to the others that he was the source of the bogus tale; they need not worry about weapon-toting birds.

But when he returned home that evening he assumed the airs of a broken man. He told his wife that the senate had discovered that his household was responsible for the breach of confidence and that he was thereby to be exiled. After apportioning to the loquacious lady a reasonable period of time in which to feel the pain of guilt and shame, he told her the truth. Plutarch concludes the anecdote by noting that the senator had tested his wife as if he were pouring water, not wine or olive oil, into a leaky jug (Plutarch *Moral Essays* 507 B–F).

Gellius (*Attic Nights* 4.5) also records the story of a not-so-innocent lie. It seems that one day a bolt of lightning wended its way earthward and struck a statue of the courageous Roman hero Horatius Cocles. Naturally the Romans viewed this phenomenon as a celestial message, so they called upon some Etruscan priests to interpret it—an odd choice, because relations between Romans and Etruscans were uneven at best.

Not surprisingly, the priests decided to provide false information to their Roman inquirers; they advised the Romans to move the statue to lower ground, a safer place where it could not as readily serve as a lightning rod.

Later, however, their intentionally giving false advice was exposed, and they were summarily executed. This event, in turn, gave rise to the following ditty, supposedly recited by children all over Rome: *Malum consilium consultori pessimum est,* "Bad advice always backfires on the adviser."

Cicero tells a tale about Tiberius Claudius Centumalus, owner of a home on the Caelian Hill. It seemed that a portion of Centumalus's house obstructed the view of priests who needed a clear sightline to the sky to observe **Shady Real Estate Deals** celestial omens. Centumalus was duly ordered to disassemble the offending parts of the structure.

Instead, the disgruntled homeowner put his house on the market and soon found a buyer: Publius Calpurnius Lanarius. Centumalus neglected to inform Lanarius of the divinely inspired directive, however; when the priests ordered Lanarius to remove the obstructions, he complied.

Lanarius's sense of religious piety and duty was severely tested when he discovered, after the fact, that Calpurnius had sold him the house knowing that a portion of it would have to be demolished. He was so incensed that he resorted to a modern-sounding solution: he demanded in court that Calpurnius reimburse him for his demolition expenses and for the loss in value of his property. And the court agreed. Calpurnius had to pay up (Cicero *On Duties* 3.66).

In another real estate deal, Cicero once wanted to buy a home on the pricey Palatine Hill but lacked the financial wherewithal to carry out the purchase. So he borrowed the money—2,000,000 sesterces—from Publius Cornelius Sulla, who was at the time under indictment for participation in the Catilinarian conspiracy, an armed revolution masterminded by the dissolute politician Catiline (d. 62 B.C.). The loan became public knowledge before Cicero was able to close on the house.

Because he was embarrassed by the subsequent political fallout—a victim of the conspiracy actually borrowing money from one of the accused conspirators!—he took refuge in a politician's favorite ploy: he stonewalled inquiries by denying any involvement. No, he had not received a loan. No, he had no intention of purchasing property on the Palatine. He added that if he ever in the future took up residence there, then his accusers would be proven correct.

Not long afterward, however, Cicero did indeed complete the Palatine deal. When once more he was called to an accounting, he merely laughed and said that his public denials of interest in the house were only intended to mislead rival bidders, in order to keep the price from escalating (Aulus Gellius *Attic Nights* 12.12).

In yet another shady real estate deal, Amoenus purchased a rather modest house for 100,000 sesterces and then went to work furnishing it with fineries. He brought in expensive couches with inlaid tortoise shells, furniture made of costly Moorish citrus wood, counters and cupboards crammed with gold and silver and a multitude of slaves. Then Amoenus decided to sell the place. Asking price: 200,000 sesterces (furnishings not included!) (Martial *Epigrams* 12.66).

Minor Malfeasance by an Elected Official   An aedile by the name of Aulus Hostilius Mancinus sued a lady of the evening—Manilia by name—because, he claimed, he had been hit in the head by stones hurled from the general direction of her apartment window. For evidence, he displayed his grievous cranial injury to the court.

Manilia fought back. She countered that Mancinus had attempted to visit her pleasure house one evening of his own free will. Knowing the consequences of entertaining a Roman official in her establishment, she refused him admittance. He persisted, retreating only when he became the target of a volley of stones.

The court ruled in Manilia's favor, determining that Mancinus, as an elected servant of the people, should have known better and that his suit was baseless (Aulus Gellius, *Attic Nights* 4.14).

SOCIAL AMUSEMENTS

Many of the most insufferable bores anywhere could be found at *recitationes*, where writers offered public **Public Readings** readings of their latest literary creations. Some of the wordsmiths could legitimately lay claim to the title, but others were mere hacks.

One of the most celebrated incidents recounted in Homer's *Odyssey* is Odysseus's encounter with—and escape from—the alluring songs of the Sirens. But Martial knew a man named Canius who was such a persistent motormouth that even Odysseus would find it difficult to escape his idle chatterings (3.64).

Another of Martial's acquaintances. Afer by name, loved to boast of his seemingly endless cash flow: 100,000 sesterces owed to him by Coranus, 200,000 by Mancinus, 300,000 by Titius, 600,000 by Albinus. He had a cool million coming from Sabinus and Serranus each. His rental properties brought him 3,000,000; his livestock, 600,000. Every time that Martial chanced upon Afer, a glowing financial report loomed ad nauseam . . . literally, Martial's suggested cure for his gastroenterological distress: Afer should pay him for listening to his ineffable infomercial (4.37).

Euclides, like Afer, talked in exaggerated terms of his money and his pedigree: 200,000 sesterces annually from his farms and other properties, and a distinguished heritage, which originated with Leda. One day, while he was loudly boasting about family and fortune, a large key tumbled out of his pocket—showing that the self-congratulating Euclides actually made his living as a lowly doorman (5.35).

Sometimes, dining pleasure might be coupled with recitation displeasure. Ligurinus occasionally invited friends to dinner, but at a price: they had to listen to his recitations. So even though the food was excellent—turbots, mullets, mushrooms, oysters—the guests had only one word for Ligurinus: *Tace!* ("Shut up!") (Martial *Epigrams* 3.45).

Another time, Martial condescended to dine with Ligurinus. The dinner unfolded thus:

Appetizers: lettuce, fish sauce, first volume of writings to be recited.

Main courses: second and third volumes get priority, while the food gets cold.

Dessert: fourth and fifth volumes come first.

Martial suggests to Ligurinus that he will dine alone in the future unless his voluminous writings are put to the best possible use: to wrap dead mackerels (3.50).

Eating and Mooching For those who could not flatter, cajole, or bribe their way into some old woman's will, there were smaller-scale freebies to be pursued—like dinner invitations.

Martial wondered in print why he had not been invited to Sextus's birthday bash, despite the fact that the two of them had been good friends for many years. Could the reason be that Martial lacked the funds to procure a worthy gift? A pound of Spanish silver, perhaps, or a new toga or cloak. Sextus's explanation for the invitation omission: "My social secretary forgot" (Martial *Epigrams* 7.86).

Sometimes—or so it appears—hosts would offer dinner invitations simply to flaunt their riches before their less affluent guests. As the recipient of a dinner invitation from the wealthy Sextus. Martial wondered whether he had been invited to eat or to envy (4.68).

In his fifth Satire, Juvenal describes at length a dinner party given by the wealth-flaunting patron Virro, a man who loved to demean his less fortunate client-guests by offering them second (or third, or fourth) class fare. Virro's two-tiered banquet could be outlined like this:

What Virro Got	*What His Guests Got*
• A gilded drinking cup studded with amber and beryl	• Cracked and leaking glass cups
• The finest servants, well bred and expensive	• A servant so vile and grim no one would want to meet him in a dark alley
• The best white bread, baked of highest quality flour	• Scraps of hard, crusty bread, of the kind that could shatter a man's incisors
• A huge lobster served with asparagus and top-of-the-line sauces and dressings	• A minuscule plate with a shrimp and half an egg, served with greens so old they would more aptly be called browns
• A mullet and lamprey, both caught near Sicily and rushed to Virro's table; goose liver and truffles	• An eel, more like a water snake, fresh from the sewers of Rome
• The most delectable mushrooms	• Moldy toadstools
• A variety of fresh fruits	• Rotten apples

Juvenal also sarcastically notes that the socially inferior guests would be well advised to refrain from making comments or complaints; to do so would result in immediate ejection from the premises: *Plurima sunt quae non audent homines pertusa dicere laena*, "There are lots of things that people with worn-out coats had better not say" (Juvenal *Satires* 5.130–131).

Seekers of free dinners could be obnoxiously persistent. Consider, for example, one Menogenes. Inescapable, that's what he was. Go to the public baths, and there he was, ready to tend to your every request. Need a shagger of missed balls during a game of catch? Ask Menogenes. Want someone to praise to the skies the whiteness of your bath towels? Menogenes will attest to their whiter-than-snow appearance even if they have most recently been used as necessary adjuncts to burping the baby. Combing the fringe of a balding pate? Menogenes will swear that even Achilles did not sport a finer head of hair. Need a little skin lotion? How about a cloth for a sweaty brow? Menogenes is the man! And Menogenes will keep on with the flattery, the praise, and the favors until he hears those magic words: "Oh, all right, you're invited to dinner!" (Martial *Epigrams* 12.82).

Philomusus hoped to earn his dinner in a manner reminiscent of Menogenean tactics. He told tall tales, some true, some fictitious. He claimed to know exactly what the Parthian king Pacorus was up to and the troop strength of the Rhenish and Sarmatian armies. He knew all about "eyes only" military messages, and how often it rained in Egypt, and how much corn would be arriving in Rome from Africa, and what wordsmith would write the next bestseller. And on and on and on. Martial would invite Philomusus to dinner on one condition: *Nil novi!* ("No news!") (9.35).

Sometimes, invitees actually declined dining opportunities. Martial lambasts an aptly named fellow, Dento, for refusing invitations not once but four times—and there was a time when Dento gladly ate at Martial's home. The reason for his newfound aloofness? *Unctiore mensa.* He had found a host with a richer table (5.44).

Compare Dento to Philo. Philo swore that he never ate at home, and it was true. Whenever he lacked a dinner invitation, Philo did not eat at all (5.47).

The orator Papius Piso had a standing rule for his slaves: speak only in answer to direct questions, and at all other times, remain quiet. It so happened that Piso had given an order that Clodius be invited to his home for dinner. When the appointed hour arrived, all the guests were present except Clodius. Piso became a little edgy; he asked the slave, to whom delivery of the invitation to Clodius had been entrusted, if Clodius had received it. When the slave replied in the affirmative, Piso wondered aloud why Clodius had yet to appear. The slave informed his master that Clodius had declined the invitation.

"Well, why didn't you tell me?!"

"Because you didn't ask me!" replied the ever-obedient slave (Plutarch *Moral Essays* 511 D, E).

Why do bad things happen to good people, or by extension, why do the good suffer while the evil prosper? This ages-old philosophical question was addressed by Catullus (Poem 47), when he lamented that his good friends Veranius and Fabullus wandered around the city streets vainly seeking a dinner invitation, whereas two scoundrels, Porcius and Socration, flaunted their wealth by holding lavish midday feasts. Life most definitely did not seem fair!

Catullus also immortalized Fabullus (Poem 13) upon the occasion of his inviting Fabullus to dinner. His friend will eat well at the poet's house only if Fabullus brings the food, the drink, the girls, the gossip. The reason? *Tui Catulli plenus sacculus est aranearum*, "Nothing but cobwebs in friend Catullus's wallet."

Martial (*Epigrams* 3.12) also had a friend named Fabullus. Want to eat at Fabullus's house? He will offer his guests the finest of perfumes and the emptiest of dinner plates. The guests may starve, but at least they will be aromatically correct in the process.

Martial often complains about the dinnertime stinginess of hosts. A certain Mancinus had invited no fewer than sixty guests to dinner, with nothing more on the menu than a boar. No grapes, no apples, no pears, no pomegranates, no cheese, no olives, no nothing! Merely a boar, and a small one at that. So small, in fact, that Martial claims it could have been carved by an "unarmed dwarf" (1.43).

Martial's acquaintance Selius had a similar problem. Martial saw him one day pacing back and forth along a public colonnade. Selius was evidently greatly distressed. His head hung low; he was beating his chest and tearing at his hair. Yet all was well with his family, he faced no financial difficulties, his worldly possessions were secure. The problem? *Domi cenat*, "He dines at home!" (2.11).

The gastronomically challenged Selius appears in another poem (2.14), where Martial describes Selius's desperate efforts to avoid a home-cooked dinner. He ran here and there, to statues, shrines, and paintings of various gods, vainly praying to them to rescue him from this culinary fate worse than death. When that ploy failed, Selius tried another tack: to accompany authors to public recitals, or lawyers to court, and loudly applaud and acclaim their verbal jousts. *Effecte*! ("Right on!") *Graviter*! ("Impressive!") *Cito*! ("Quick thinking!") *Euge*! ("Way to go!") *Beate*! ("Super!") The Selian flattery continued until, at long last, the flatteree uttered the magic words: *Facta est iam tibi cena; tace!* "Okay, you've got your dinner; now shut up!"

Martial often invited Gallus to dinner, but the favor was never returned, even though Gallus often tendered dinner invitations to others. Still, Martial forgave him. Why? Because Martial was soft-hearted and because a hard-hearted person like Gallus deserved a little sympathy (3.27).

Sometimes, an unwelcome would-be dinner guest caused Martial more than passing annoyance. He speaks spitefully of one Charopinus, who habitually hung around his home when the cooking fires were burning, ready to accost Martial if no invitation was forthcoming (5.50).

Cantharus, on the other hand, saved his verbal jabs until after he had wangled a dinner invitation—wherupon he threatened and cursed his fellow diners (9.10).

Martial's friend Caecilianus incurred the poet's wrath for a related but different reason: food thievery. It seems that Caecilianus, when invited to Martial's dinner party, brought along a doggie bag big enough to feed a dozen dogs: portions of sow's udder, a pork chop, a chicken drumstick, a pigeon, a half mullet and a whole bass—all these goodies and more Caecilianus took from Martial's table (2.37).

Martial also describes, although he does not name, a one-eyed dinner thief whom he compares to Autolycus, the patron god of purloiners. This thief could snatch cups and spoons, napkins and mantles, cloaks and lamps. On those rare occasions when he returned home empty-handed, he still could not retire for the evening before stealing his own sandals from the slave that was supposedly guarding them (8.59).

Catullus (Poem 12) tells the tale of Asinius Marrucinus, napkin-thief supreme, who plied his dubious trade at a party apparently given by Catullus. Marrucinus, however, made the mistake of pilfering a napkin that had a certain sentimental value: it was a gift from two close friends. In an effort to retrieve his property, the poet threatened the perpetrator with a sort of "pen-is-mightier-than-the-sword" ultimatum: either return the napkins, or fall victim to 300 measures of acerbic Catullan poetry!

Catullus was also victimized by a certain Thallus, who stole from him not only a napkin but also a cloak and some writing tablets. To add insult to injury, Thallus openly displayed these items at his own home. Catullus (Poem 25) promised to Thallus a painful fate if his property was not given back: a flogging.

But the best of the napkin thieves was the light-fingered Hermogenes, the pre-eminent purloiner of unguarded tableware, the Harry Houdini of lifting linens. He was so skilled at his "trade" that even if a fellow diner watched his right hand while holding his left, Hermogenes could figure a way to nab a napkin.

He even stole napkins in non-dining environments. For example, during gladiatorial shows, spectators sometimes waved handkerchiefs as signs of approval for a wounded gladiator. At one such occasion, Hermogenes managed to liberate four of these hankies from their rightful owners.

At some dinner parties where Hermogenes was on the guest list, neither host nor invitees furnished napkins, for fear of Hermogenes and his thieving ways. In those instances, he stole the tablecloths or even the valances from the couches.

Spectator areas at amphitheaters were often shaded on hot days by large awnings. But when Hermogenes was spotted in the crowd, the awnings were immediately rolled up and packed away. Sailors in port quickly stowed their vessel's sails if Hermogenes happened to be strolling past.

In short, Hermogenes always realized a net gain in linen ownership whenever he attended a dinner party (Martial *Epigrams* 12.29).

ANECDOTES ABOUT DAILY LIFE

What a Deal! Bassus strutted about town decked out in an expensive Tyrian cloak, one worth 10,000 sesterces—a real steal, one might say, because Bassus had no intention of paying for it (Martial *Epigrams* 8.10).

Bad Hair Day Anyone who hoped to avoid an early grave should likewise avoid the overly enthusiastic barber Antiochus. The sawbones Alcon was gentler when excising a hernia or amputating a hand. Prometheus (who was chained to a rock and forced to expose his constantly regenerated liver to the ravages of an eagle) would actually have preferred the bird's talons to Antiochus's clippers. Pentheus (who was dismembered by his crazed mother) would have chosen the maternal touch over Antiochus's professional services. A customer who allowed Antiochus to shave him would look like a boxer who had just gone twelve rounds with an ancient version of Mike Tyson. Only he-goats were wise; they *kept* their beards (Martial *Epigrams* 11.84).

Marinus, on the other hand, would no doubt have had his share of bad hair days, if only he had more hair. He was a bald man who let the fringes of his hairless pate grow long enough that he could comb them over the top, thus appearing to have a full head of hair. But as soon as a gust of wind blew, the hairs of Marinus's quasi-toupee returned to their accustomed places on the sides of his head. Martial's advice: admit that you're old, Marinus, and quit trying to give the appearance of two people (10.83).

Hold Your Tongue, Lady! Free speech certainly was not free, at least in the case of Claudia, daughter of Appius Claudius Caecus, the censor under whose leadership the Appian Way was built.

As Claudia was leaving the theater one day, she was shoved, jostled, and generally handled roughly by the exiting crowd. Angered, she blurted out that she might have been killed, had it not been for the actions of her brother, the naval commander Publius Claudius Pulcher. (His incompetence in battle in 249 B.C. had led to the deaths of thousands of sailors; Claudia's tactless point: if those men had survived and had attended the theater that day, their numbers, added to the other theatergoers, would have crushed her to death.)

She added insult to indiscretion by loudly expressing the wish that her brother could return to life and lead another fleet to its doom, this one composed of all those knockabouts who had pushed and elbowed her at the theater exit.

Such sentiments were too much for the crowd to bear. Claudia was summoned to appear before the aediles Gaius Fundarius and Tiberius Sempronius, who fined her 25,000 pounds of bronze coins (Aulus Gellius *Attic Nights* 10.6).

Luxurious Lollia Paulina

Lollia Paulina lived in the mid first century A.D. and traveled with some very fast company. The granddaughter of the super-wealthy Marcus Lollius, crony of Augustus and first Roman governor of Galatia, she married the emperor Caligula in 38—only to find herself divorced the following year. A few years later she tried to wangle a second imperial marriage for herself, this one with the emperor Claudius. But the desired merger never took place.

Pliny the Elder mentions that he once saw Lollia Paulina at an engagement party, where she was decked out with emeralds and pearls literally covering her head, neck, and fingers. The total value of the baubles: 40,000,000 sesterces. And she had documentation to prove rightful ownership. The source of all this glitter and glitz? Not an imperial benefaction, but an inheritance from her grandfather—the spoils of his Galatian plunderings (Pliny the Elder *Natural History* 9.117–118).

Blinded by the Light?

Marcus Bucculeius, a man called by Cicero *homo neque meo judicio stultus et suo valde sapiens*, "not a fool in my judgment, and pretty darn smart, in his," had a house for sale. He found a willing buyer, a certain Lucius Fufius. Fufius, however, apparently demanded a clause in the selling agreement that gave him "all rights to light." After the transaction was completed and Fufius had moved into his new house, he constantly hounded Bucculeius with legal actions; anytime a new structure went up in any part of Rome, no matter how far it might be from Fufius's house, if that new building blocked any portion of his view, no matter how minute, he sued Bucculeius for breach of contract (Cicero *On the Orator* 1.179). Cicero does not say whether the suits succeeded, and Bucculeius is not mentioned in any other sources.

Acquittal by Crying

Cicero recounts an anecdote from a second century B.C. courtroom in which Servius Sulpicius Galba was being prosecuted on some charge (not specified by Cicero). To play on the sympathies of the judges and the spectators, Galba brought into court with him a young child named Quintus, a close relative. This Quintus he would carry around the room, almost piggy-back style, until the boy began to whimper. And then Galba loudly asserted that he had entrusted the fate of his own two young sons "to the guardianship of the nation," should he be convicted and, presumably, exiled from Rome. All these heartstring-tugging words and actions had the desired effect: Galba, even though generally disliked and even hated by many people, gained an acquittal.

Cicero quotes Cato's summary of the case: *nisi pueris et lacrimis usus esset, poenas eum daturum fuisse,* "If [Galba] had not resorted to using children and tears, he would have paid the price [for his crime]." Another legal observer, Publius Rutilius Rufus, noted that exile or even death was preferable to the employment of such devious courtroom tactics. But they worked for Galba (Cicero *On the Orator* 1.227–228).

A Twin-Killer of a Deal The slave dealer Toranius pulled off a nifty deception on Mark Antony. Toranius owned a pair of handsome slave boys who appeared to be identical twins. The asking price—200,000 sesterces—was very steep, but so desirous was Antony of possessing the boys that he paid the dealer's "sticker price."

Later, however, he discovered that he had been duped. The two boys turned out not to be identical twins after all; their very different speech patterns gave them away. One came from Asia, the other from north of the Alps. Their facial resemblance was mere coincidence.

Antony was furious. He tracked down Toranius to complain about the deception and, in particular, the inflated price he had paid for the pair.

Evidently Toranius was expecting a visit from Antony, because he had a ready reply. He claimed that the price was high for the very reason that inspired Antony's complaint: namely, that although identical twins were relatively common, it was most unusual that two boys from virtually opposite ends of the earth would look so much alike. This actually increased their value; far from being cheated, Antony got a great deal, at least according to Toranius.

Antony must have bought the salesman's pitch because, although angry when he first accosted Toranius, he left happy (Pliny the Elder *Natural History* 7.56).

Mark Antony Was No Angel Whether the context be Mark Antony's public or private life, Plutarch reports that many noble Romans hated him for "his ill-timed drunkenness, his heavy expenditures, his debauches with women, his spending the days in sleep or in wandering about with crazed and aching head, the nights in revelry or at shows, or in attendance at the nuptial feasts of mimes and jesters." At one of these bachelor parties—in honor of the impending wedding of a mime named Hippias—Antony stayed up all night swigging liquor. Early the next morning he managed to stagger down to the forum, fortunately accompanied by a friend who held open Antony's toga; otherwise, Antony would have decorated the public square with his vomiting (Plutarch *Life of Mark Antony* 9; tr. Bernadotte Perrin, LCL).

Pliny the Elder reports that a certain senator named Struma Nonius owned a ring containing an opal the size of a hazelnut; its estimated value was 2,000,000 sesterces. So desirous was Mark Antony of obtaining the ring that he proscribed Nonius. When that unfortunate senator fled from Rome, the only possession he took with him was the very ring so coveted by Antony (Pliny the Elder *Natural History* 37.81).

The Covetous Mark Antony

In 212 B.C. the shocking case of two war profiteers came to light. The two men in question were Marcus Postumius and Titus Pomponius Veientanus. According to Livy, Postumius "had no equal in dishonesty and avarice in the state, except Titus Pomponius Veientanus."

Skulduggery on the Seas

Their scam worked as follows. The Roman government underwrote private shipowners' losses at sea, if the shipowners were conveying in their vessels arms and supplies for the Roman army. Postumius and Veientanus became skilled in falsifying accounts of shipwrecks and therefore collecting money for ships "lost" at sea, even though in many instances the ships never existed.

But even in the cases of ships that actually had been wrecked, skulduggery lurked. The two men would load worthless cargo into delapidated ships and then send them out to sea and deliberately sink them (providing, of course, life boats for the crews). They would then file their claims with the government, asserting that the lost ships and cargo were of great value.

Eventually their chicanery was exposed, and a fine of 200,000 *asses* was imposed on Postumius. (Veientanus had been taken prisoner in the meantime by the Carthaginians and hence was unable to share his partner's fate.) Postumius at first attempted to appeal the fine to the popular assembly, but later he decided that such a public hearing might not be in his best interests. So he quietly left Rome and disappeared into voluntary self-exile (Livy *From the Founding of the City* 25.3–4).

Plutarch relates a story that illustrates the boundless wealth of Lucius Licinius Lucullus. A certain (unnamed) praetor was hoping to make a name for himself by sponsoring a lavish stageplay for potential voters. So he went to the house of Lucullus to ask him for the use of some purple cloaks, which were needed for costuming certain of the actors. Lucullus told the praetor that he would look around and that the man should return the following day.

Take All You Want

When the next day dawned, the praetor returned, whereupon Lucullus asked him how many cloaks he needed. When the praetor replied "100,"

Lucullus told him that he could have twice as many (Plutarch *Life of Lucullus* 39).

Hannibal's Cattle Trick
The Carthaginian commander Hannibal made one of his few errors in 217 B.C., when maneuvering his army near the town of Casilinum. Because of his unfamiliarity with the area, he unwisely led his troops into a narrow valley surrounded by steep hills. Fabius Maximus, leader of the Roman army that had been shadowing Hannibal, immediately saw a golden opportunity. Quickly they occupied the heights with heavily armed soldiers while simultaneously springing a sneak attack on the rear of the Carthaginian column. When Hannibal became aware of his army's predicament he wanted to retreat, but retreat was rendered impossible by Roman control of the high ground. So there sat the Carthaginians, easy prey for the Romans, until Hannibal came up with a trick.

In the course of their marches around Italy the Carthaginians had captured numerous herds of cattle. Hannibal ordered about 2,000 of these animals to be driven together; next, he directed his men to gather sticks and twigs, tie them into 2,000 bundles, and attach one bundle to each bovine head. This done, they waited for nightfall.

As soon as it was dark, the Carthaginians set fire to the 2,000 bundles of sticks and began to herd the cattle toward the valley passes, with the army following closely. When the Romans on the heights viewed this spectacle from a distance, they thought that the army was on the march, by torchlight.

As long as the fire was consuming only the kindling, the cattle shuffled along in orderly fashion. But when the flames reached the heads and ears of the animals, they panicked with pain and fear and began running madly in wild confusion. Many of them lumbered toward the wooded hillsides, where they started numerous forest fires when their burning heads came into contact with dry tinder.

Viewing this latest helter-skelter display of torchlight, the Roman guards became terrified. They did not know how to interpret what met their eyes, except to surmise that the Carthaginian army was mounting a night attack. They assumed the worst, panicked again, and deserted their posts. As soon as Hannibal realized that the Romans were fleeing, he ordered his own men to occupy the newly vacated heights, while the rest of the army escaped unscathed from the confined valley.

Meanwhile, Fabius Maximus figured out the trick, because some of the singed cattle had been captured by his soldiers. However, he was reluctant to move against the Carthaginians in the dark, fearing ambushes or additional Hannibalian chicanery. At daybreak the Romans pursued the retreating Carthaginians, who turned on their pursuers and inflicted some serious losses on them.

When the news of Hannibal's escape reached Rome, the senate and many other government officials, especially the tribunes, heaped abuse on Fabius Maximus for being outsmarted by his Carthaginian counterpart. The incident ultimately led to an odd and unprecedented arrangement in which Fabius was required to share his dictatorial power with his former underling, Marcus Minucius (Plutarch *Life of Fabius Maximus* 6–10).

In the mid first century B.C. the Roman scene was graced by a beautiful woman named Praecia. Her charming attractiveness soon earned her a wide circle of friends. Those who entertained political ambitions found a willing and capable ally in Praecia.

Praecia and Political Power

One of these friends, Cethegus, fell completely under her influence. She helped him attain the political power he craved, but once he achieved it he conducted public business in the manner that she dictated. Later she became the friend and companion of Lucius Licinius Lucullus, who used his association with her to obtain support from Cethegus.

Lucullus's infatuation with Praecia ended when he obtained a governorship in the province of Cilicia, through the joint efforts of Cethegus and Praecia, and thus had no further use for her feminine wiles (Plutarch *Life of Lucullus* 6).

REFERENCES

Aulus Gellius: *Attic Nights.*
Catullus: *Poems.*
Cicero: *Letters to His Friends; On Duties; On the Orator*
CIL 5.3325; 6.10047; 6.10048; 6.10051; 6.10053; 6.10056; 6.10063; 6.10177; 6.10196; 10.7297.
Julius Caesar: *Gallic Wars.*
Juvenal: *Satires.*
Livy: *From the Founding of the City.*
Martial: *Epigrams.*
Pliny the Elder: *Natural History.*
Pliny the Younger: *Letters.*
Plutarch: *Life of Fabius Maximus; Life of Lucullus; Life of Mark Antony; Moral Essays.*

10

Religion

ROMAN RELIGION

Roman religion was a complex and sometimes confusing mixture of priesthoods, cults, superstitions, omen interpretation, deities and religious festivals honoring those deities. Overseeing the machinery of the religious establishment was the *pontifex maximus* ("chief priest"). His duties and prerogatives were many and varied, including supervision of the calendar, which conferred upon him, among other powers, the right to manipulate the date on which elections were held. He exercised a general supervision over all other priests and priestly colleges, and although his office entailed no specific legislative or governmental responsibilities, his advice on public policy issues was usually respected.

Other priestly groups included the fifteen augurs, whose primary responsibility was to determine the will of the gods, as manifested in various avian forms such as flight patterns, cries, or feeding habits. A famous case of augury ignored occurred in 249 B.C., during the First Punic War. The Roman naval commander Publius Claudius Pulcher, eager for battle, ordered that the sacred chickens be brought onto the deck of his ship, and be offered their meal of corn. Should the birds eagerly devour their food, it would be deemed a propitious sign for the commencement of hostilities. Should they refuse to eat, or eat only half-heartedly, the gods' advice was thought to be *alio die*, "another day" for the battle.

Not once, but on two occasions, the sacred chickens showed no enthusiasm for consuming their corn. Finally, the exasperated Pulcher ordered them to be tossed overboard, simultaneously exclaiming "If they won't eat, then let them drink!" Thereupon, he initiated an attack on the Carthaginians, with the predictable result: a nearly total destruction of the Roman fleet (Battle of Drepanum).

Assigned to cultivate the shrine and the worship of the hearth goddess Vesta were the six Vestal Virgins. Vestal Virgins were selected at a very young age—6–10. They were required to serve for a period of thirty years, during which time they had to remain chaste. Should they violate the celibacy rule, they might be stoned to death, or buried alive. During their thirty-year commitment, it was expected that Vestal Virgins would spend the first ten years learning their duties, the second ten years performing them, and the third ten years training new candidates.

Vestal Virgins enjoyed numerous perquisites; whenever they ventured out in public, they were accompanied by state-sponsored bodyguards. They were granted choice seating at public games or entertainments. Because of the respect they commanded, they might be entrusted with important public or private documents for safekeeping. If a condemned criminal happened to see a Vestal Virgin while en route to his punishment, he was granted an immediate pardon.

Of the numerous festivals dotting the Roman calendar during the course of the year, one of the most interesting was the Lupercalian, celebrated every February 15. On that day, scantily clad young men—the Luperci—ran around the Palatine Hill armed with leather whips, with which they struck any women whom they encountered. These proceedings were generally thought to ensure both fertility for the women who were lashed, and also a good beginning for the upcoming planting season, and subsequent harvest later in the year.

One of the Luperci for the 44 B.C. celebration of the festival was Mark Antony. As was his custom, he had imbibed too freely in alcoholic spirits, so when he happened across his good friend Julius Caesar, he jokingly tried to place a crown on Caesar's head. Although Caesar resisted, the damage to his public image was done; onlookers assumed that Antony's gesture was not an empty one, and that Caesar's rumored desire for kingship was real.

One month later, Caesar lay dead, the victim of the famous Ides of March assassination, an event precipitated in part by the Lupercalian "crowning."

The Roman pantheon was filled with a wide array of gods and goddesses; the most powerful was the patron deity of Rome, Jupiter. His epithet *Optimus Maximus* ("best [and] greatest") indicates the regard that the Romans had for him. Other noted members of the pantheon included Juno, Jupiter's wife and consort; Mars, god of war; Minerva, goddess of wisdom; Neptune, god of the earth and sea. Janus, the god of beginnings and the guardian of gates, was generally depicted with two heads, or faces, since a gate or a door faces both inside and out. Janus was also associated with the beginning of the new year; the first month of the Roman year, *mensis Januarius*, was named for him, and this Roman belief persists to the present day, in the etymological connection of the name of our first month to the Latin *Januarius*.

CURSES

A curse in ancient Rome was much like its modern counterpart: a verbal or written wish that evil befall the person against whom the curse was directed. A large number of the written versions—*tabellae defixionis*—have survived. The following example is dated to the mid first century B.C.:

O wife of Pluto, good and beautiful Proserpina . . . pray tear away from Plotius health, body, complexion, strength, faculties. Consign him to Pluto, your husband. May he be unable to avoid this by devices of his. Consign that man to the fourth-day, the third-day, the every-day fever. May they wrestle and wrestle it out with him, overcome and overwhelm him unceasingly until they tear away his life. So I consign him as victim to thee, Proserpina, unless, O Proserpina, unless I ought to call thee Goddess of the Lower World.

Send, I pray, someone to call up the three-headed dog with request that he may tear out Plotius's heart. Promise Cerberus that thou wilt give him three offerings—dates, dried figs, and a black pig—if he has fulfilled his task before the month of March. All these, Proserpina Salvia, will I give thee when thou hast made me master of my wish. I give thee the head of Plotius, slave of Avonia. O Proserpina Salvia, I give thee Plotius's forehead. Proserpina Salvia, I give thee Plotius's eyebrows. Proserpina Salvia, I give thee Plotius's eyelids. Proserpina Salvia, I give thee Plotius's eye-pupils. Proserpina Salvia, I give thee Plotius's nostrils, lips, ears, nose, and his tongue and teeth so that Plotius may not be able to utter what it is that gives him pain; his neck, shoulders, arms, fingers, so that he may not be able to help himself at all; his chest, liver, heart, lungs, so that he may not be able to feel what gives him pain; his abdomen, belly, navel, sides, so that he may not be able to sleep; his shoulder-blades, so that he may not be able to sleep well; his sacred part, so that he may not be able to make water; his buttocks, thighs, legs, shins, feet, ankles, soles, toes, nails, that he may not be able to stand by his own aid.

Should there so exist any written curse, great or small—in what manner Plotius has, according to the laws of magic, composed any curse and entrusted it in writing, in such manner I consign, hand over to thee, so that thou mayest consign and hand over that fellow, in the month of February. Blast him! Damn him! Blast him utterly! Hand him over, consign him, that he may not be able to behold, see, and contemplate any month further! (*CIL* 1.2520; tr. E. H. Warmington LCL)

OMENS

Omens seen prior to the Battle of Philippi (42 B.C.)

Omen	Where Seen
1. changes in the size of the sun, sometimes very small, other times gigantic; once seen nocturnally	Rome
2. random thunderbolts	Rome
3. meteors	Rome
4. sounds of nonexistent battles, heard at night	Rome
5. A dog dragging a dead dog to the temple of Ceres, and burying it there	Rome
6. miraculous birth: a child with ten fingers on each hand	Rome
7. miraculous birth: a mule bearing a sort of hybrid offspring, half horse and half mule	Rome
8. ceremonial chariot of Minerva spontaneously smashed to bits by an unknown force	Rome
9. rivers flowing backward	Rome/environs
10. swarms of bees in the camp of Cassius	Macedonia
11. during a purification ceremony, an attendant placed a garland backward on Cassius's head	Macedonia
12. during a procession of soldiers, one of the marchers, a small boy, stumbled and fell	Macedonia
13. screeching vultures circled Cassius's camp	Macedonia

The emperor Augustus (ruled 27 B.C.–A.D. 14) benefitted from two auspicious dreams. In one, a Thessalian dreamt that the assassinated Julius Caesar commanded him to report to Augustus and tell him that he should wear something that he (Julius) had worn while alive. So Augustus placed one of Julius's rings on his finger and often wore it after the battle of Philippi.

In the second dream, Augustus's physician dreamt that Minerva directed him to insist that Augustus be personally present in the front lines of the battle, even though Augustus was quite ill at the time. But he took the advice and survived the battle (Dio Cassius 47.41).

VESTAL VIRGINS

A Vestal Who Forgot the Formula
In 123 B.C. a young Vestal Virgin named Licinia dedicated an altar, a small shrine, and a ceremonial couch at a temple of the Bona Dea on the Aventine Hill. Unfortunately, she forgot to consult the chief priests on the propriety of such a dedication. Ultimately the pontifex maximus, Publius Mucius Scaevola, nullified Licinia's consecretory acts, claiming that her failure to gain his blessing and that of his priestly colleagues justified his ruling (Cicero *On His Own House* 136).

The Vestal Virgin Tuccia (thought to have lived in the third century B.C.) was implicated for unchastity by an unnamed accuser. When the time came for Tuccia to respond to the charges, she said that she would exonerate herself not by words but by this remarkable deed:

A Hole in the Bucket—But No Leak

After gaining the court's approval, she made her way to the Tiber River: Dionysius of Halicarnassus, the source of the story, says that the entire citizenry of Rome accompanied her. When she arrived at the river bank she dipped a sieve into the water, filled it, and carried it back to the forum. Not a drop leaked out.

Her innocence thus proven, the ire of the court and the crowd turned toward her accuser. But he had already fled the scene, and no trace of him was ever discovered (Dionysius of Halicarnassus *Roman Antiquities* 2.69).

In 204 B.C. the worship of the eastern cult goddess Cybele was introduced into Rome. A ship bearing her images and accoutrements was making its way up the Tiber River when it became stranded on a sand bar.

Claudia and the Power of Prayer

When Claudia saw what had happened, she decided to take matters into her own hands by physically freeing the craft from its predicament. This she was able to do after first publicly praying that the feat would be possible only if her virginity was still intact—which apparently it was (Suetonius *Life of Tiberius* 3).

Appius Claudius Pulcher—there were several of them, but we are concerned with the one who was consul in 143 B.C.—had achieved some mixed military results while campaigning against the Salassi, an Alpine tribe. Upon

Claudia and Filial Devotion

his return to Rome, however, he expected to be granted a triumphal procession. When his request was rejected, he went ahead with the parade plans on his own initiative. A tribune tried to put a halt to the procession, but at that point the Vestal Virgin Claudia—by some accounts, Claudius's sister; by others, his daughter—jumped into her kinsman's chariot and accompanied him the rest of the way. The prestigious presence of the Vestal rendered irrelevant the tribunician objections. (The story of the devoted Vestal Virgin Claudia is recounted by several authors, most notably Suetonius *Life of Tiberius* 3 and Cicero *Pro Caelio* 34.)

The year 216 B.C. was a bad one for the Romans. Worst was the utter humiliation at the Battle of Cannae, where some 50,000 Roman legionnaires were slain on one hot afternoon in August by Hannibal's Carthaginians; the disaster touched virtually every family in the city.

Two More Vestals Who Strayed

Besides that, many omens were observed, including the conviction of two Vestal Virgins—Opimia and Floronia—of unchastity. Their timing could not have been worse for an already demoralized populace.

Both died violent deaths—one by her own hand, the other by being buried alive, the prescribed punishment in such cases. The young man who caused Floronia to stray, Lucius Cantilius, a pontifical secretary, was so brutally flogged that he died as a result (Livy 22.57).

REFERENCES

Cicero: *On His Own House; Pro Caelio*.
CIL 1.2520.
Dio Cassius: *Roman History*.
Dionysius of Halicarnassus: *Roman Antiquities*.
Livy: *From the Founding of the City*.
Suetonius: *Life of Tiberius*.

11

Retirement

Retirement was a roll of the dice for many older Romans. In an era in which private pensions were rare and government assistance nonexistent, many were unable to live out their golden years with gold enough to match in their savings.

SOME LONGEVITY RECORDS

Pliny the Elder (*Natural History* 7.48) provides some remarkable examples of very long-lived Romans:

Name	Place of Residence	Age
Lucius Terentius	Bononia	135
Marcus Aponius	Rimini	140
Tertulla	Rimini	137
Marcus Minucius Felix	Veleia	150
Marcus Perperna	Rome	98
Marcus Valerius Corvinus	Rome	100
Livia (not Augustus's wife)	Rome	97
Statilia	Rome	99
Terentia (wife of Cicero)	Rome	103
Galeria Copiola	Rome	104

Sammula	Rome	110
Clodia (wife of Ofilius)	Rome	115
Titus Fullonius	Bononia	150

THE ROMANS AT THE END OF THEIR WORKING LIVES

Most Romans could not look forward to a lavish retirement lifestyle. Social Security was unknown: pension plans were rare, and those that did exist were generally inadequate. Yet the concept of a time of leisure at the end of a work-filled life appealed to many.

The kinds of questions that nag modern prospective retirees—When can I retire? Where will I retire? Can I afford it? How will I spend my time?—also confronted the ancient Romans. Then, as now, a variety of answers emerged.

Interestingly, the age of 60 was something of a milestone, the time when many Romans, especially public servants, began to shed their official duties and obligations. At that age Roman senators were permitted to retire, and citizens in general were excused, or perhaps prohibited, from voting. There was even a proverb—*sexagenarios de ponte*, "60-year-olds off the bridge!"—that referred to preventing sexagenarians from passing across the walkway (or "bridge") that led to the polling place. (A more literal, although less likely, interpretation: throw 60-year-olds off a Tiber bridge and into the river, to drown them!)

Few Romans could look forward to an early retirement replete with a pension. Soldiers, however, were one notable exception. Under the emperor Augustus, legionnaires could retire after twenty years of service and receive a lump sum payment of 12,000 sesterces. Members of the praetorian guard—soldiers who served as imperial bodyguards and orderlies—fared better. They could retire after sixteen years and receive a payment of 20,000 sesterces.

Land was frequently given to retiring soldiers instead of money, and it is likely that many former soldiers found second careers as farmers after leaving the army.

An Unusual Pension Plan In the summer of 70 B.C. a remarkable trial took place in ancient Rome. Had daily newspapers existed in those days, this trial would have made headlines; it would have been accorded prime-time coverage had there been television and radio.

It seems that a certain Gaius Verres had behaved most abominably while serving as the Roman provincial governor of Sicily in the years 73 to 71. He had extorted money, stolen precious artworks, absconded with fabrics and tapestries, and taken large amounts of grain, honey, and household furnishings; in short, he had plundered the province. Upon his return to Rome, he was tried for these crimes.

The prosecutor was Marcus Tullius Cicero. For his defense, Verres hired the best known attorney of the time, Quintus Hortensius. Verres and Hortensius undoubtedly anticipated a favorable outcome, especially because the Roman government often winked at evidence of fraud and abuse in its provincial governors.

However, they had not foreseen the degree of skill and energy that Cicero would bring to the proceedings. In the opening arguments he built such a damning case against Verres that the corrupt bureaucrat skipped town before the conclusion of the trial. Verres fled to Massilia (modern Marseilles), where, it is said, he lived in comfortable retirement for some twenty-seven years, until his death in 43. His golden years were no doubt financed by his ill-gotten Sicilian wealth (Cicero *Against Verres* passim).

Seneca (4 B.C.–A.D. 65) recounts the story of one Sextus Turannius, who had worked for many years as the head of the corn supply (*praefectus annonae*), up to the age of 90; and even then, he would have stayed on the job had he not been forced into retirement by the emperor Caligula. So closely did Turannius identify life with work that he went home, laid down on his bed, and ordered his entire household to mourn him as if he had died. He kept up this odd behavior until finally the emperor rescinded his retirement orders and allowed Turannius to return to work (Seneca *On the Shortness of Life* 20; Tacitus *Annals* 11.31; Tacitus records his *praenomen* as Gaius).

What Age Retirement?

A semi-legendary character with the imposing Roman name of Lucius Quinctius Cincinnatus underwent a rather startling metamorphosis from soldier to farmer to soldier and back to farmer. This Cincinnatus had retired to a small farm near Rome. One day (in 458 B.C.), while he was in the midst of digging a ditch, a delegation of handsomely attired Roman senators made their way across his dusty fields with a message and a request for the old man. The Roman army was under seige; no capable military leaders could be found in Rome to deal with the impending disaster. Would he, Cincinnatus, come out of retirement to organize an attempt to rescue the trapped men?

Retired . . . Unretired . . . Retired Again

Cincinnatus dropped his spade, donned his toga, and accompanied the senators to the city, where he assumed the office of dictator. He quickly marshaled a force, marched to the scene of the entrapment, extricated the army, and returned to Rome in triumph. Sixteen days after becoming dictator, he resigned his office and retired (a second time!) to his farm (Livy *From the Founding of the City* 3.26).

In the second century A.D. the charioteer Appuleius Diocles retired from the track at age 42 after an outstanding 24-year career in which he won 1,462 races. An inscription bearing his name turned up at the fashionable little town of Praeneste (about 20 miles southeast of Rome); apparently

A Charioteer's Retirement

Diocles selected Praeneste as the place for his retirement, which was made financially secure by the millions of sesterces he had earned as a chariot driver. Presumably other successful charioteers also retired in their forties, or even their thirties, and used their often substantial winnings as their pension fund (*CIL* 14.2884).

Gladiatorial Retirees   Gladiators who performed creditably over an unspecified period of years were given a *rudis*, a wooden sword symbolizing the completion of their service. After retiring from gladiatorial combat, some found jobs as trainers or coaches. Others sometimes hired themselves out for special occasions. Early in his reign, the emperor Tiberius (ruled A.D. 14–37) sponsored gladiatorial shows to commemorate his father and grandfather; he induced several retired gladiators to perform. The lavish stipend that Tiberius offered these gladiators—100,000 sesterces—probably had something to do with their decision to return to the arena.

Other gladiators, however, had no interest in staging comebacks once they had retired. The poet Horace (*Epistles* 1.1.) tells of a gladiator by the name of Veianius who, upon his retirement, hung up his equipment in a shrine of Hercules, thereby rendering it inaccessible when his friends urged him to resume his career.

He Stayed Past His Prime   Stories abound in the modern world of professional athletes who continue to try to play competitively long after their skills have declined. Quintilian relates the story of Domitius Afer, an orator who displayed the same kind of stubbornness. Quintilian considered Afer to have been the best orator that he ever knew; and yet; in his later years Afer continued to speak in court although his eloquence had significantly diminished, a sad fact of life obvious to everyone except Afer himself. Thus, when Afer gave public speeches, some of his listeners snickered and smirked, while others blushed with embarrassment over the once great orator's verbal missteps.

Quintilian suggests that this was the point at which Afer—or any orator, for that matter—ought to retire. In retirement, he could still remain mentally active by reading, writing, and advising and instructing younger colleagues who might wish to consult him. "For what is more worthwhile than to teach that which you know well?" (Quintilian *Institutes of Oratory* 12.11).

Not the Retirement He Expected   In his younger days, the poet Ovid (43 B.C.–A.D. 17) envisioned retiring to his familial estate, tending the house and fields, enjoying the company of his wife and friends. Even worn-out ships "retire" to the peace and quiet of the harbor, he notes, and as for old chariot race horses? They find themselves "retired" too, in pastures, leisurely dining on meadow grass.

But pleasant days such as these did not await Ovid in his later years, which saw him exiled to the Black Sea area. He notes the irony: when young, he expected to work and struggle, thus earning a comfortable span of retirement years when he was old. But his life unfolded in precisely the opposite manner (Ovid *Tristia* 4.8).

Circumstances conspired to prevent many well-known Romans from ever enjoying a peaceful retirement, even though most of them had enough money to live out their final years in comfort and security. One of the most influ- **No Rest for the Weary** ential politicians in Roman history, Cato the Elder, continued to harangue the Roman senate with his thunderous oratory well after he had marked his eightieth birthday. Julius Caesar was in the midst of drafting and proposing a series of government reforms when he was struck down by assassins. Cicero's distinguished career ended ignominiously in the proscriptions of 43 B.C. Augustus long dreamt of retirement, a dream that was never to be realized; he was still on the job when he died at the age of 76.

Sometimes, the selection of a suitable place for retirement caused marital friction. The first century A.D. poet Statius addressed his wife, Claudia, in a lengthy poem in which he praised the virtues of Naples as a retirement community: a **"No" to a Neapolitan Retirement** temperate climate, an unhurried lifestyle, easy access to Mediterranean resort towns, ready availability of cultural and recreational activities. Claudia, it seemed, preferred the hustle and bustle of life in Rome; a move to the more sedate Naples did not appeal to her (Statius *Forests* 3.5).

ENJOYING RETIREMENT

Seneca wryly notes that people caught up in the hustle and bustle of their careers think in only vague terms of retirement. "I'll hang it up when I turn 50," they might say, or "When I'm 60, that's when I pay my last visit to the office." Living life to the fullest, he suggests, should be of greater concern (Seneca *On the Shortness of Life* 3).

Pliny the Younger recounted a typical day in the life of a former statesman named Spurinna. This Spurinna customarily arose early in the morning and took a 3-mile walk. He then relaxed, and occasionally did some **Perambulation, Play, Poetry, Parties** reading, before boarding his chariot for a brisk, 7-mile ride. After that invigorating experience he walked another mile and then rested again or turned his attention to writing. According to Pliny, Spurinna penned excellent poetry, in both Greek and Latin.

In the afternoon a swim was followed by a rigorous game of handball, activities that Spurinna thought helped him to ward off the infirmities that often come with old age. After bathing, he relaxed for a time before consuming a nourishing but modest dinner. He particularly enjoyed the company of dinner guests, and he frequently socialized with them far into the night.

His retirement lifestyle must have served him well, for when Pliny wrote about him, Spurinna was in his seventy-eighth year and still going strong.

In another letter, addressed to a retired friend by the name of Pomponius Bassus, Pliny recounted the pleasant routine that Bassus enjoyed: living in an agreeable place, swimming and exercising at any time the spirit moved him, entertaining friends, reading. It seemed to Pliny entirely appropriate that a sexagenarian like Bassus, who had devoted the prime of his life to civic affairs, should in his later life rightly deserve a period of peace and quiet (Pliny the Younger *Letters* 4.23).

Living Off the Fat of the Villa   Seneca reminisces about a retired millionaire named Servilius Vatia, who retreated to his sumptuous country villa to pass his golden years in luxurious self-absorption. Those still active in the political arena would, after suffering some setback or catastrophe, exclaim: "Oh, Vatia, you're the only one who knows how to live!" Seneca, however, claims that Vatia was better at hiding than living, and that there is a world of difference between *otium* ("retirement") and *ignavia* ("laziness"). Seneca himself would never pass by Vatia's estate without thinking *Vatia hic situs est*, "Vatia lies here" (Seneca *Moral Epistles* 55).

A Literary Retirement   In a short letter to Atticus, Cicero implores him to prepare certain unnamed things for his (Cicero's) anticipated retirement. But Cicero does specify one pleasure to which he looked forward in retirement: a personal library.

Interestingly, this letter is dated 67 B.C. (when Cicero was 39 years of age), at least twenty years before he might be expected to consider retiring. So it appears that the prudent Cicero was planning well in advance for his hoped-for years of leisure (Cicero *Letters to Atticus* 1.7).

Work Is Existing; Retirement Is Living!   Gaius Sulpicius Similis, a centurion whom the emperor Hadrian promoted to praetorian prefect, felt honored by that exalted rank but also a bit uneasy, as he was near retirement age. So, after holding the post for a short time, he resigned even though Hadrian wanted him to stay on. Similis, it is said, retired to a quiet life in the country. When he died seven years later, this epitaph was carved on his tombstone: "Similis lies here. He existed for a number of years; he lived for seven years" (Dio Cassius *Roman History* 69.19).

Surprises from a Retired Soldier   In a letter to his friend Caninius Rufus, Pliny the Younger writes about Terentius Junior, a retired soldier. Pliny hints that Terentius could have enjoyed additional career advancement but instead chose to withdraw to his country estates and a slower lifestyle. This Terentius invited Pliny to dinner; Pliny prepared for the inevitable mealtime conversation by thinking about and rehearsing the topics that he thought might interest a soldier-turned-gentleman-farmer. But he was surprised when his host initiated a scholarly exchange on Greek and Roman literary topics. Pliny was so impressed by the range and scope of Terentius's knowledge that it almost seemed that the man lived in Athens, not in an Italian country farmhouse. Pliny came away from the evening with a newfound respect for retirees of Terentius's background and breeding (Pliny the Younger *Letters* 7.25).

Tiberius Catius Silius Italicus enjoyed a distinguished career as a lawyer and provincial governor, and he also **A Politician's** held the consulship (in A.D. 68). When he retired from **Retirement** public life a rich man, he devoted himself to two pursuits: acquiring property, and writing. He bought several homes in Campania and liberally furnished them with books and works of art. He also devoted much of his retirement to writing, eventually producing the longest poem (over 12,000 lines) in the Latin language: *Punica*, an epic about the Second Punic War.

Plagued by ill health, he committed suicide in A.D. 101 at the age of 75 (Pliny the Younger *Letters* 3.7; cf. Martial *Epigrams* 7.63 and 11.48).

Long before his ascension to the emperorship in A.D. 14, Tiberius unexpectedly decided to withdraw from **Early Retirement** public life; the date was 6 B.C., when he was only about 35 years of age. This move was especially unusual because Tiberius was, as Suetonius puts it, "at the flood-tide of success ... in the prime of life and health." Speculation ran rampant in Rome about the reason for Tiberius's sudden retirement; he himself said that he made the move to avoid seeming to be a threat to more direct claimants to succeed Augustus as emperor.

In any event Tiberius journeyed to Ostia, where he boarded a ship and sailed along the coast of Campania; from there he went to the island of Rhodes, where he followed an unpretentious lifestyle. Included in his routine were strolls through the local gymnasium and visits with philosophers and their students.

He remained in Rhodes for eight years until returning to Rome in A.D. 2, and "unretiring" (Suetonius *Life of Tiberius* 10–14; tr. J. C. Rolfe LCL).

REFERENCES

Cicero: *Against Verres; Letters to Atticus; On Old Age.*
CIL 14.2884.
Dio Cassius: *Roman History.*
Horace: *Epistles.*
Livy: *From the Founding of the City.*

Martial: *Epigrams*.
Ovid: *Tristia*.
Pliny the Elder: *Natural History*.
Pliny the Younger: *Letters*.
Quintilian: *Institutes of Oratory*.
Seneca: *Moral Epistles; On the Shortness of Life*.
Statius: *Forests*.
Suetonius: *Life of Tiberius*.
Tacitus: *Annals*.

Appendix: Roman Authors

This section contains brief biographies of all ancient authors whose works were consulted in the preparation of the text. The general format: common name; formal Roman name; the author's major works, along with brief synopses; a short and perhaps little known "factoid" about the author.

Appian (Appianus, ca. A.D. 95–ca. 165)

Place of birth: Alexandria, in Egypt.

Major work: *Roman History*, which includes accounts of the Punic wars, the second century B.C. wars in Spain, the Mithridatic wars, the Syrian wars, and the first century B.C. Roman civil wars.

Factoid: Appian's friend Marcus Cornelius Fronto wrote a (still extant) letter of recommendation on his behalf to the emperor Antoninus Pius (reigned A.D. 138–161), regarding Appian's appointment to a government administrative post (procurator). The effort succeeded.

Apuleius (ca. A.D. 123–?)

Place of birth: Madaurus, in Africa.

Major work: *Metamorphoses*, also known as *The Golden Ass*, in which the protagonist, Lucius, is transformed into a donkey; as such, he undergoes many adventures, before ultimately being restored to human form.

Factoid: The youthful Apuleius married Pudentilla, a wealthy old widow, which laid him open to charges of using magic to induce the old woman to agree to the marriage. He defended his behavior in a still extant speech, *Apologia*.

Aulus Gellius (ca. A.D. 123–ca. 169)

Place of birth: unknown; possibly Africa, or even Rome.

Major work: *Attic Nights* (*Noctes Atticae*), 398 short essays, divided into 20 books, on an interesting mix of historical, linguistic, military, legal, and social topics.

Factoid: In his preface, Gellius says that he wrote his essays for the entertainment of his children, and that the title came to him during a year-long sojourn in Athens. When he was a young student he began compiling his material during the long winter nights there, hence, "Attic nights."

Ausonius (Decimus Magnus Ausonius, ca. A.D. 310–ca. 394)

Place of birth: Bordeaux.

Major works: Numerous poems and letters; his masterpiece is considered to be *The Moselle* (*Mosella*), a poem about the river of the same name.

Factoid: Ausonius taught rhetoric for thirty years in Bordeaux, until—at an age when most people (then as now) begin contemplating retirement—he embarked upon a second career as a politician; a move facilitated by his role as tutor to the future emperor Gratian (reigned A.D. 367–383). In 379, at the age of about 70, he attained the consulship.

Cato the Elder (Marcus Porcius Cato, 234–149 B.C.)

Place of birth: Tusculum.

Major work: *On Agriculture* (*De Agri Cultura*), a manual on farming that considered virtually every aspect of the topic, from buildings and equipment, to crops and livestock, to veterinary practices, to hiring farmhands, to harvest sacrifices.

Factoid: According to Plutarch, Cato earned his third name later in life, because of the high esteem in which he was held by the Romans, Cato deriving from the Latin adjective *catus*, "shrewd," or "prudent."

Catullus (Gaius Valerius Catullus, 84–54 B.C.)

Place of birth: Verona, in northern Italy.

Major work: 113 lyric poems, on a variety of social, interpersonal, and mythological topics.

Factoid: Catullus mingled with Rome's first century rich and famous. He had a torrid love affair with the well-connected Clodia; and he knew Julius Caesar, although he felt no compunction about occasionally lampooning the great Caesar in his poetry.

Celsus (Aulus Cornelius Celsus, fl. early first century A.D.)

Place of birth: unknown.

Major work: *On Medicine* (*De Medicina*), which includes information on anatomy, surgery, pharmacology, treatments, and medical history.

Factoid: Very little is known about Celsus' life, perhaps because he may not have been all that highly regarded by his own contemporaries. Quintilian, for example, refers to him as a *vir mediocri ingenio*, "a man of modest talent."

Cicero (Marcus Tullius Cicero, 106–43 B.C.)

Place of birth: Arpinum, southeast of Rome.

Major works: Numerous published orations, fifty-eight of which survive intact or virtually intact; philosophical essays; over 900 letters written by or to him. The outstanding orator and prose author of his time—perhaps of *any* time in Roman history—it would be impossible to single out any one of his works as the most noteworthy. However, he is perhaps best remembered for the four emotionally-charged speeches he delivered against the violent revolutionary Catiline, in November and December of 63.

Factoid: Cicero served as a government official (*quaestor*) in Sicily during the year 75. He felt quite proud of his work there, and he was certain that news of his accomplishments was a daily topic of conversation back in Rome. So he was very deflated when, en route home after his Sicilian year, he came across an old acquaintance, who asked him where he had been and what he had been doing for the last year.

Dio Cassius (Cassius Dio Cocceianus, ca. A.D. 155–after 229)

Place of birth: Nicaea, in Bithynia.

Major work: *Roman History*, covering well over 1,000 years, from the time of Aeneas' arrival in Italy, down to Dio's own time.

Factoid: Near the end of his long career, devoted equally (it seems) to literature and public service, Dio incurred the displeasure of a clique of government officials, and so decided to retire to his native Nicaea. He claimed, however, that foot problems, not political pressure, prompted him to return home.

Diodorus Siculus ("the Sicilian," fl. first century B.C.)

Place of birth: Agyrium, in Sicily.

Major work: *Library of History* (*Bibliotheca*), a world history, covering events in Egypt, Asia, India, Assyria, Arabia, Ethiopia, Libya, Greece, Sicily, and Italy.

Factoid: While visiting Egypt, Diodorus saw an angry mob demand the execution of a Roman diplomat simply because he had accidentally killed a cat, an animal sacred to the Egyptians.

Dionysius of Halicarnassus (fl. late first century B.C.)

Place of birth: Halicarnassus, in modern southwestern Turkey.

Major work: *Roman Antiquities*, a historical survey covering Rome's origins to the beginning of the First Punic War (264 B.C.).

Factoid: Although Dionysius hailed from a Greek-speaking city and wrote in Greek, he spent twenty-two years in Rome, immersing himself in the language and culture, and researching historical details, to add to the authenticity of his writing.

Horace (Quintus Horatius Flaccus, 65–8 B.C.)

Place of birth: Venusia, southeast of Rome.

Major works: *Odes* (*Carmina*); *Epodes*; *Satires* (*Sermones*); *Epistles* (*Epistulae*); *Art of Poetry* (*Ars Poetica*); *Poem for the Secular Games* (*Carmen Saeculare*). Horace's poetry touches upon a wide variety of topics; the *Satires* are the best sources of information about various aspects of Roman daily life.

Factoid: Horace provided a unique self-assessment in the first book of *Epistles*: "I was a freedman's son . . . I found favour, both in war and peace, with the foremost of the state; of small stature, grey before my time, fond of the sun, quick in temper, yet so as to be easily appeased" (1.20.20 ff; tr. H. Ruston Fairclough).

Juvenal (Decimus Junius Juvenalis, ca. A.D. 60–ca. A.D. 130)

Place of birth: Aquinum, about 80 miles southeast of Rome.

Major work: Sixteen caustic *Satires*, on Roman life and society.

Factoid: Although Juvenal's literary reputation has soared in modern times, he was not well known in his own time, and the only contemporaneous author who even mentions him is Martial.

Livy (Titus Livius, 59 B.C.–A.D. 17)

Place of birth: Patavium, modern Padua, in northern Italy.

Major work: *From the Founding of the City* (*Ab urbe condita*), a history of Rome from its foundation to Livy's own time; a massive work, 35 of its 140 books are extant.

Factoid: Livy spent over forty years of his life working on this book, beginning around 29 B.C.

Lucretius (Titus Lucretius Carus, ca. 99 B.C.–ca. 55)

Place of birth: unknown; possibly Rome.

Major work: *On the Nature of Things* (*De Rerum Natura*), in six books, on epicureanism.

Factoid: According to St. Jerome's biography of Lucretius, he went insane after having consumed a love potion; he wrote *De Rerum Natura* during occasional periods of clear-headedness.

Macrobius (Ambrosius Theodosius Macrobius, fl. early fourth century A.D.)

Place of birth: possibly Egypt; all that is known for certain is that he was not born in Italy.

Major work: *Saturnalia*, in seven books, an account of a dinner party at which the guests discuss numerous topics: literature, social life, food and drink, money, mythology, etc. The work contains much anecdotal information about Roman life.

Factoid: Macrobius dedicated *Saturnalia* to his son, Eustachius, because he believed that of all the relationships possible in human life, none was stronger than parental love.

Martial (Marcus Valerius Martialis, ca. A.D. 40–ca. 104)

Place of birth: Bilbilis, in Spain.

Major works: Fourteen books of *Epigrams*, expressing his (often humorous) views on Roman life and people. He also authored *The Book of Spectacles* (*Liber Spectaculorum*), to commemorate the opening of the Coliseum.

Factoid: Martial emigrated to Rome around 64, and lived there for the next thirty-five years, before returning to his native Spain, where he remained until his death.

Ovid (Publius Ovidius Naso, 43 B.C.–A.D. 17)

Place of birth: Sulmo, in central Italy.

Major works: *Metamorphoses; Art of Love* (*Ars Amatoria*); *Love Poems* (*Amores*); *Sad Poems* (*Tristia*); *Letters from Pontus* (*Epistulae ex Ponto*). His masterpiece: *Metamorphoses* is an epic collection of mythological stories, all involving some sort of change of form or shape.

Factoid: Just before Ovid learned that he was to be exiled from Rome (A.D. 8), he burned his manuscript copy of *Metamorphoses*. Fortunately, however, friends also had copies, and they saw to it that the poet's greatest work was published.

Persius (Aulus Persius Flaccus, A.D. 34–62)

Place of birth: Volaterrae, north of Rome.

Major work: One book of six *Satires*, on religion, literature, and philosophy.

Factoid: Modern critics sometimes tend to downgrade Persius' literary abilities, but the ancient assessments were kinder. Quintilian and Martial were both impressed with his work; Martial wrote that Persius was more often mentioned for his one little collection of satires than was Domitius Marsus (an Augustan-era poet) for his epic masterpiece *Amazonis*.

Petronius (Petronius Arbiter, fl. first century A.D.)

Place of birth: unknown.

Major work: *Satyricon*, a fragmentary novel containing the famous description of the elaborate dinner party given by the nauseatingly pompous Trimalchio.

Factoid: Petronius eventually ran afoul of one of emperor Nero's courtiers (Tigellinus), who persuaded Nero to order Petronius to commit suicide. Petronius duly obeyed, but got the last laugh in his will, in which he ridiculed Nero and his associates for their vices and perversions.

Plautus (Titus Maccius Plautus, ca. 255–184 B.C.)

Place of birth: Sarsina, north of Rome.

Major works: Plautus is thought to have written about 130 comedy plays, of which 20 survived.

Factoid: The popular film and play *A Funny Thing Happened on the Way to the Forum* is loosely based on Plautus' play *The Bragging Soldier* (*Miles Gloriosus*).

Pliny the Elder (Gaius Plinius Secundus, A.D. 23–79; uncle of Pliny the Younger)

Place of birth: Comum, in northern Italy.

Major work: *Natural History* (*Naturalis Historia*), in thirty-seven books, a vast compendium of information on nearly every known aspect of the natural world.

Factoid: Pliny proclaims in the preface to *Natural History* that the work contains 20,000 facts gleaned from 2,000 books by 100 authors.

Pliny the Younger (Gaius Plinius Caecilius Secundus, A.D. 62–ca. 112; nephew of Pliny the Elder)

Place of birth: Comum, in northern Italy.

Major works: 247 letters (*Epistulae*) to friends, and an oration, *Panegyricus*, praising the emperor Trajan.

Factoid: Pliny was in the vicinity of Mount Vesuvius when it erupted in 79; in two of his 247 letters (both addressed to the historian Tacitus), Pliny graphically detailed his observations of the tragedy.

Plutarch (ca. A.D. 50–ca. 120)

Place of birth: Chaeronea, in Greece.

Major works: Fifty biographies of noted Greeks and Romans; seventy-eight *Moral Essays* (*Moralia*). Both the biographies and the essays contain much information about Greek and Roman society.

Factoid: Although Plutarch was a sophisticated and educated man who traveled widely, he never lost touch with his small town roots, and spent most of his life in his native Chaeronea.

Procopius (fl. sixth century A.D.)

Place of birth: Caesarea, in Palestine.

Major work: *History of the Wars of Justinian*, primarily a survey of Justinian's military campaigns against the Persians, Vandals, and Goths.

Factoid: Although Procopius was principally a military historian, he also wrote a detailed and incisive work on art and architecture: *Justinian's Buildings*.

Propertius (Sextus Propertius, ca. 50 B.C.–ca. 16)

Place of birth: Assisi.

Major work: Four books of *Elegies*, many of which revolve around his relationship with his enamorata, whom he called Cynthia in the poems (although her real name was Hostia).

Factoid: In the first elegy of Book IV, Propertius claims to be the Roman Callimachus (Callimachus having been regarded as the best Greek elegiac poet). Such a boast brought him the enmity of older, more established Roman poets, especially Horace.

Quintilian (Marcus Fabius Quintilianus, ca. A.D. 35–ca. 90)

Place of birth: Calaguris, in Spain.

Major work: *Institutes of Oratory* (*Institutio Oratoria*), in which he discusses the theory and practice of oratory and education, as well as sections devoted to literary criticism.

Factoid: Quintilian was the first educator in Rome to receive a salary from the state.

Scriptores Historiae Augustae (SHA), "imperial historians"

The SHA was a kind of consortium of six writers who authored biographies of the Roman emperors, from Hadrian (reigned A.D. 117–138) through Carus and his sons (late third century A.D.). The two *scriptores* from whom information was gleaned for this book:

Aelius Spartianus (*Life of Hadrian*).

Julius Capitolinus (*Life of Marcus Aurelius; Life of Pertinax*).

Seneca (Lucius Annaeus Seneca, ca. 4 B.C.–A.D. 65)

Place of birth: Corduba, in Spain.

Major works: *Moral Epistles* (*Epistulae Morales*), 124 letters to his friend Lucilius, on a variety of ethical and philosophical topics; *Dialogues* (*Dialogi*), philosophical essays. He also wrote plays, scientific essays, and an interesting satire on the deification of the emperor Claudius, *Apocolocyntosis*.

Factoid: According to Dio Cassius, Seneca's advanced literary and oratorical skills so incurred the jealousy of the emperor Caligula that (in A.D. 39), he was on the brink of ordering Seneca's execution. The emperor relented only because he believed that Seneca (whose health was never robust) would soon die of natural causes.

Sidonius Apollinaris (Gaius Sollius Apollinaris Sidonius, ca. A.D. 430–ca. 480)

Place of birth: Lugdunum, modern Lyon, in France.

Major works: *Poems* (*Carmina*); *Letters* (*Epistulae*). Most of the entries in both collections were addressed to friends or relatives.

Factoid: In 456, Sidonius recited a poem that he had written in honor of Avitus, the new emperor. For this public act of loyalty, Avitus ordered a statue of the poet to be placed in Trajan's forum in Rome.

Suetonius (Gaius Suetonius Tranquillus, ca. A.D. 69–A.D. 140)

Place of birth: unknown.

Major works: *Lives of Illustrious Men* (*De Viris Illustribus*); *Lives of the Caesars* (*De Vita Caesarum*); the latter is a series of biographies of the first twelve Roman emperors.

Factoid: Suetonius owned a bronze statuette of Augustus, depicting him as a boy. He later gave the figure to the emperor Hadrian, who prized it highly.

Tacitus (Cornelius Tacitus, ca. A.D. 55–ca. 117)

Place of birth: unknown.

Major works: *Annals* (*Annales*), covering Roman history from A.D. 14–68; *Histories*, covering 69–96; *Agricola*, a biography of his father-in-law; *Germania* (*Germany*), a description of Germany; *Dialogue on Oratory* (*Dialogus*), an oratorical treatise.

Factoid: Although primarily remembered as a historian, Tacitus was also a skilled orator/lawyer. In A.D. 100, he and his close friend Pliny the Younger prosecuted the ex-governor Marius Priscus for extortion. They won the case; Priscus was directed to repay to the treasury the 700,000 sesterces he had stolen, and then to go into exile.

Tibullus (Albius Tibullus, ca. 55–19 B.C.)

Place of birth: unknown.

Major work: Two books of elegaic love poems, fourteen entries in all.

Factoid: The poet Horace addressed a poetic *Epistle* (1.4) to Tibullus, in which he referred to Tibullus' estate at Pedum, an upscale community near Rome. Tibullus evidently enjoyed a comfortable, serene, and slow-paced lifestyle when in Pedum.

Varro (Marcus Terentius Varro, 116–27 B.C.)

Place of birth: Reate, northeast of Rome.

Major works: *On the Latin Language* (*De Lingua Latina*); *On Agriculture* (*De re rustica*). The former work emphasizes vocabulary and etymology, the latter, all aspects of farming.

Factoid: Varro lost his property and nearly his life in the proscriptions of 43. But he survived, and continued his literary pursuits all the way to the time of his death, at age 89.

Velleius Paterculus (ca. 19 B.C.–after A.D. 30)

Place of birth: unknown.

Major work: *Compendium of Roman History* (*Historiae Romanae*), a survey of Roman history from its earliest beginnings, down to his own time.

Factoid: After a lengthy military career, Velleius seems to have retired from the army around A.D. 15, and to have devoted much of the rest of his life to his historical writing; some critics have hence accused him of (literary) dilettantism.

Vergil (Publius Vergilius Maro, 70–19 B.C.)

Place of birth: near Mantua, in northern Italy.

Major works: *Georgics*, on farming; *Eclogues*, pastoral poems; and his epic masterpiece about the founding of the Roman race, *Aeneid*.

Factoid: Although Vergil had gained great fame as a poet even in his own time, he was shy and reclusive. Suetonius notes that whenever Vergil visited Rome—which he seldom did—he would scurry into the nearest house whenever people on the street recognized him.

Vitruvius (Vitruvius Pollio, fl. during the time of Augustus)

Place of birth: unknown.

Major work: *On Architecture* (*De Architectura*), in ten books, covering topics such as qualifications for an architect, city planning, construction methods and materials, public and private structures, pavements.

Factoid: Vitruvius was apparently not a man of immense ego, for he described himself as short, not very handsome, and weakened by bad health.

Bibliographic Essay

Although the works of ancient authors have been the major sources of information for this book, the wide array of works by modern authors also deserves grateful acknowledgment.

The scholars and editors who have produced the Loeb Classical Library (LCL) of translations of Greek and Roman authors would be a good starting point; no one has done more to make classical literature accessible to specialists and generalists alike than these talented individuals. For the benefit of readers who may have never consulted a Loeb volume, the following information is typically found:

- a biography of the author
- a synopsis of that author's major works
- a review of the manuscript tradition
- a bibliography of modern scholarship pertaining to the author
- the text itself, with the Latin or Greek on the verso (even-numbered) pages and the English translation on the facing pages
- annotations for both the ancient language text and the translation
- an index

Of the hundreds of translations that have been made of the works of classical authors, the versions in the Loeb Classical Library come the closest of fulfilling the charge facing any translator: "as free as possible, as literal as necessary." It would be difficult to find translations anywhere that are as true to the ancient texts, while at the same time as readable, as those contained in the LCL.

The following Loeb Classical Library editions were consulted in the preparation of this book. Most (if not all) Loeb volumes have undergone numerous reprintings; in each case, only the date of the first printing appears in the bibliography. All references to Cambridge refer to the Massachusetts location.

Anderson, W.B. Sidonius Apollinaris *Poems and Letters*. Cambridge and London, 1936.

Bailey, D.R. Shackleton. Martial *Epigrams*. Cambridge, 1993.

Basore, John W. Seneca *Moral Essays* (including *On Firmness; On Anger*), Vol. I. Cambridge and London, 1928.

———. Seneca *Moral Essays* (including *On Tranquility of Mind*), Vol. II. Cambridge and London, 1932.

Bennett, Charles E. Horace *The Odes and Epodes*. Cambridge and London, 1914.

Butler, H.E. Propertius *Elegies*. London and Cambridge, 1912.

———. Quintilian *Instituto Oratoria*. London and New York, 1921.

Cary, Earnest. Dio *Roman History*. London and New York, 1914.

———. *The Roman Antiquities of Dionysius of Halicarnassus*. London and Cambridge, 1937.

Cornish, Francis W. Catullus *Poems*. Cambridge and London, 1913.

Dewing, Henry B. Procopius *History of the Wars*. London and New York, 1914.

Duff, J. Wight, and Arnold M. Duff. *Minor Latin Poets* (including *Panegyric on Piso*). Cambridge and London, 1934.

Fairclough, H. Rushton. Horace *Satires, Epistles and Ars Poetica*. Cambridge and London, 1926.

———. Virgil *Aeneid*. Cambridge and London, 1918.

Foster, B.O. Livy *Ab Urbe Condita*, Vol. I. Cambridge and London, 1919.

———. Livy op. cit. Vol. III. London and Cambridge, 1924.

———. Livy op. cit. Vol. IV. London and New York, 1926.

———. Livy op. cit. Vol. V. Cambridge and London, 1929.

Granger, Frank. Vitruvius *On Architecture*. Cambridge and London, 1931.

Greenwood, L.H.G. Cicero *The Verrine Orations*. London and New York, 1927.

Gummere, Richard M. Seneca *Epistulae Morales*. Cambridge and London, 1917.

Hanson, John Arthur. Apuleius *Metamorphoses*. London and Cambridge, 1989.

Heseltine, Michael (rev. E.H. Warmington). Petronius *Satyricon*. London and New York, 1913.

Hodge, H. Grose. Cicero *The Speeches* (including *Pro Cluentio*). Cambridge and London, 1927.

Hooper, William D. (rev. Harrison B. Ash). Marcus Porcius Cato *On Agriculture*; Marcus Terentius Varro *On Agriculture*. Cambridge and London, 1934.

Jackson, John. Tacitus *The Annals*. Cambridge and London, 1931.

Jones, W.H.S. Pliny [the Elder] *Natural History*, Vol. VIII. London and Cambridge, 1963.

Kent, Roland G. Varro *On the Latin Language*. London and Cambridge, 1938.

Ker, Walter C.A. Martial *Epigrams*. London and New York, 1919.

Magie, David. *The Scriptores Historiae Augustae*. Cambridge and London, 1921.

Miller, Walter. Cicero *De Officiis*. Cambridge and London, 1913.

Moore, Clifford H. Tacitus *The Histories Books I–III*. Cambridge and London, 1925.

Mozley, J.H. Ovid *The Art of Love* (etc.). Cambridge and London, 1929.

Oldfather, C.H. Diodorus Siculus *Library of History*, Vol. III. London and Cambridge, 1939.

Perrin, Bernadotte. Plutarch *Life of Numa* (et al.), Vol. I. London and Cambridge, 1917.

———. Plutarch *Life of Cato the Elder; Life of Lucullus* (et al.), Vol. II. London and Cambridge, 1914.

———. Plutarch *Life of Fabius Maximus; Life of Crassus* (et al.), Vol. III. London and Cambridge, 1916.

———. Plutarch *Life of Coriolanus* (et al.), Vol. IV. London and Cambridge, 1916.

———. Plutarch *Life of Pompey* (et al.), Vol. V. London and Cambridge, 1917.

———. Plutarch *Life of Cicero* (et al.), Vol. VII. London and Cambridge, 1919.

———. Plutarch *Life of Cato the Younger; Life of Sertorius* (et al.), Vol. VIII. Cambridge, 1919.

———. Plutarch *Life of Marius; Life of Mark Antony* (et al.), Vol. IX. Cambridge, 1920.

———. Plutarch *Life of Gaius Gracchus* (et al.), Vol. X. London and Cambridge, 1921.

Peterson, Sir William. Tacitus *A Dialogue on Oratory*. Cambridge and London, 1914.

Postgate, J.P. Tibullus *Poems*. London and Cambridge, 1913.

Rackham, H. Cicero *De Fato; Paradoxa Stoicorum* (etc.). Cambridge and London, 1942.

———. Pliny [the Elder] *Natural History*, Vol. II. Cambridge, 1942.

———. Pliny op. cit. Vol. III. London and Cambridge, 1940.

———. Pliny op. cit. Vol. IV. London and Cambridge, 1945.

———. Pliny op. cit. Vol. V. Cambridge and London, 1950.

Radice, Betty. Pliny [the Younger] *Letters and Panegyricus*. Cambridge and London, 1969.

Ramsay, G.G. Juvenal and Persius. Cambridge and London, 1918.

Rolfe, John C. Aulus Gellius *The Attic Nights*. London and New York, 1927.

———. Suetonius *Lives of the Caesars; Lives of Illustrious Men* (including *On Grammarians*). Cambridge and London, 1913.

Rouse, W.H.D. Lucretius *De Rerum Natura*. Cambridge and London, 1924.

Sage, Evan T. Livy *Ab Urbe Condita*, Vol. XI. London and Cambridge, 1936.

Sage, Evan T., and Alfred C. Schlesinger. Livy *Ab Urbe Condita*, Vol. XII. London and Cambridge, 1938.

Shipley, Frederick. Velleius Paterculus *Compendium of Roman History*. Cambridge and London, 1924.

Spencer, W.G. Celsus *De Medicina*. London and Cambridge, 1935.

Sutton, E.W., and H. Rackham. Cicero *De Oratore: Books I, II*. Cambridge and London, 1942.

Walton, Francis. Diodorus Siculus, Vol. XI. London and Cambridge, 1967.

Watts, N.H. Cicero *De domo sua* (etc.). London and New York, 1923.

———. Cicero *The Speeches* (including *Pro Scauro*). Cambridge and London, 1931.

Wheeler, Arthur L. Ovid *Tristia: Ex Ponto*. Cambridge and London, 1924.

White, Horace. Appian *Roman History*. London and New York, 1912.

Williams, W. Glynn. Cicero *The Letters to his Brother Quintus* (etc.). London and Cambridge, 1954.

————. Cicero *The Letters to his Friends*. London and New York, 1927.

Winstedt, E.O. Cicero *Letters to Atticus*. London and New York, 1912.

Of nearly equal importance is *The Oxford Classical Dictionary* (OCD), a highly reliable and informative reference book. Three editions have now seen the light of day, with each edition being a marked improvement over the previous one; the most recent was published in 1996. Much of the material in the introductions to each of the chapters in *Daily Life of the Ancient Romans* was drawn from *The Oxford Classical Dictionary*.

One of the OCD's precursors, *Harper's Dictionary of Classical Literature and Antiquities*, contains much useful material, although the work is now over 100 years old.

A very handy collection of synopses of the major works of Greek and Roman authors is Lillian Feder's *Apollo Handbook of Classical Literature*. This book contains biographical sketches of the authors as well as information about editions and translations.

A truly amazing reference work is T.R.S. Broughton's *The Magistrates of the Roman Republic* (MRR), in three volumes. Broughton has listed all known office holders for every year of the Roman Republic, from 509 to 31 B.C., as well as extensive compilations of ancient references to the office holders. The MRR is a sine qua non for anyone who wishes to gain a thorough knowledge of the political environment of the Roman Republic.

As mentioned in the Introduction, there has been a profusion of books about Roman social history. To select one of these as the best is almost impossible. One candidate would have to be J.P.V.D. Balsdon's *Life and Leisure in Ancient Rome*. Not only is Balsdon's book comprehensive and highly readable, but it is heavily annotated, thereby providing the reader with numerous citations of additional sources and references. (For example, Chapter VIII, "Holidays at Home," has an astounding 475 endnote references, and many of these notes contain not one but multiple citations.)

An older, but equally well documented, source on Roman daily life is Ludwig Friedlaender's four-volume *Roman Life and Manners under the Early Empire* (the English translation of his monumental *Sittengeschichte Roms*). An informative two-volume collection of translated original sources—many pertaining to issues of daily life—is *Roman Civilization: Selected Readings* by Naphtali Lewis and Meyer Reinhold; Volume I covers the Republic; Volume II, the Empire.

Numerous general surveys on Roman history abound on the shelves of even the most limited libraries. Of the many excellent books available, the one on which I rely is M. Cary's *A History of Rome*, a detailed and well-annotated work. Chester G. Starr's *A History of the Ancient World*, and his shorter and more elementary *The Ancient Romans*, are also useful.

Selected Bibliography of Modern Works

Balsdon, J.P.V.D. *Life and Leisure in Ancient Rome.* New York, 1969.

Bonner, Stanley F. *Education in Ancient Rome.* Berkeley and Los Angeles, 1977.

Bradley, K. R. *Slavery and Society at Rome.* Cambridge and New York, 1994.

Broughton, T.R.S. *The Magistrates of the Roman Republic* (Vol. I, 509 B.C.–100 B.C.; Vol. II, 99 B.C.–31 B.C.). New York, 1951–1952.

Cary, M. *A History of Rome* (2nd ed.). New York, 1954.

Feder, Lillian. *Apollo Handbook of Classical Literature.* New York, 1964.

Frank, Tenney, and T.R.S. Broughton. *An Economic Survey of Ancient Rome.* Baltimore, 1933.

Friedlaender, Ludwig. *Roman Life and Manners under the Early Empire* (translated from the German by J. H. Freese et al.; 7th ed.). New York, 1908.

Gruen, Erich. *The Last Generation of the Roman Republic.* Berkeley and Los Angeles, 1974.

Harper's Dictionary of Classical Literature and Antiquities. New York, 1898.

Harris, H. A. *Sport in Greece and Rome.* Ithaca (NY), 1972.

Lewis, Naphtali, and Meyer Reinhold. *Roman Civilization: Selected Readings* (Vol. I, *The Republic*; Vol. II, *The Empire*). New York, 1951–1955.

Matz, David. *An Ancient Rome Chronology.* Jefferson, NC, 1997.

The Oxford Classical Dictionary. Oxford, London, and New York, 1949; 2nd ed., 1970; 3rd ed., 1996.

Starr, Chester G. *The Ancient Romans.* New York, 1971.

———. *A History of the Ancient World* (3rd ed.). New York, 1974.

Zimmerman, J. E. *Dictionary of Classical Mythology.* New York, 1964.

Index

About the Author

DAVID MATZ is Associate Professor, Humanities, at Saint Bonaventure University.

Age Smart

Discovering the Fountain of
Youth at Midlife and Beyond

Jeffrey Rosensweig, Ph.D.

Betty Liu

PEARSON
Prentice
Hall

Upper Saddle River • New York • London • San Francisco • Toronto • Sydney
Tokyo • Singapore • Hong Kong • Cape Town • Madrid
Paris • Milan • Munich • Amsterdam

Vice President and Editor-in-Chief: Tim Moore
Executive Editor: Jim Boyd
Editorial Assistant: Susie Abraham
Development Editor: Russ Hall
Associate Editor-in-Chief and Director of Marketing: Amy Neidlinger
Cover Designer: Solid State Graphics
Managing Editor: Gina Kanouse
Project Editor: Kayla Dugger
Copy Editor: Deadline Driven Publishing
Senior Indexer: Cheryl Lenser
Proofreader: San Dee Phillips
Senior Compositor: Gloria Schurick
Manufacturing Buyer: Dan Uhrig

© 2006 by Jeffrey Rosensweig and Betty Liu
Publishing as Prentice Hall
Upper Saddle River, New Jersey 07458

Prentice Hall offers excellent discounts on this book when ordered in quantity for bulk purchases or special sales. For more information, please contact U.S. Corporate and Government Sales, 1-800-382-3419, corpsales@pearsontechgroup.com. For sales outside the U.S., please contact International Sales, 1-317-581-3793, international@pearsontechgroup.com.

Company and product names mentioned herein are the trademarks or registered trademarks of their respective owners.

Printed in the United States of America

First Printing April, 2006

ISBN 0-13-186762-8

Library of Congress Cataloging-in-Publication Data

Rosensweig, Jeffrey A., 1957-

Age smart : discovering the fountain of youth at midlife and beyond / Jeffrey Rosensweig and Betty Liu.

p. cm.

ISBN 0-13-186762-8 (hardback : alk. paper) 1. Middle-aged persons—Life skills guides. 2. Retirement—Planning. 3. Old age—Planning. 4. Aging. I. Liu, Betty. II. Title.

HQ1059.4.R67 2006

646.7'9—dc22

2005036345

Pearson Education LTD.
Pearson Education Australia PTY, Limited.
Pearson Education Singapore, Pte. Ltd.
Pearson Education North Asia, Ltd.
Pearson Education Canada, Ltd.
Pearson Educatión de Mexico, S.A. de C.V.
Pearson Education—Japan
Pearson Education Malaysia, Pte. Ltd.